Best Practices of Catholic Pastoral and Finance Councils

Best Practices of Catholic Pastoral and Finance Councils

Charles E. Zech
Mary L. Gautier
Robert J. Miller
Mary E. Bendyna, RSM

Our Sunday Visitor Publishing Division
Our Sunday Visitor, Inc.
Huntington, Indiana 46750

Nihil Obstat
Msgr. Michael Heintz, Ph.D.
Censor Librorum

Imprimatur
✠ Kevin C. Rhoades
Bishop of Fort Wayne-South Bend
March 2, 2010

Copyright © 2010 by Charles E. Zech, Mary L. Gautier, Robert J. Miller, and Mary E. Bendyna, RSM. Published 2010.

15 14 13 12 11 10   1 2 3 4 5 6 7 8 9

ISBN 978-1-59276-720-5 (Inventory No. T1041)
LCCN: 2009943274

Interior design by M. Urgo
Cover design by Rebecca J. Heaston
Cover photo by Shutterstock

PRINTED IN THE UNITED STATES OF AMERICA

Contents

Acknowledgments

This study had its genesis with a series of discussions among Charles Zech, Director of Villanova University's Center for the Study of Church Management (CSCM); Dr. Mary Bendyna, RSM, the Executive Director of the Center for Applied Research in the Apostolate at Georgetown University (CARA); Dr. Mary Gautier, Senior Research Associate at CARA; and Dr. Robert Miller, Director of the Office of Research and Planning for the Archdiocese of Philadelphia and a member of the boards of both the CSCM and CARA. These discussions focused on the complementarities of skills available at these two centers to study parish-level issues.

Subsequently, the Center for the Study of Church Management received a research grant from a foundation that wishes to remain anonymous to study parish advisory councils, with the proviso that CARA would be a partner in the research project. The authors are grateful to this foundation for the confidence they've shown to the CSCM and CARA, both through the awarding of this grant and previous grant awards to both organizations. Clearly, this project could not have been completed without their financial support.

We are grateful to the many pastors, parish staff members, parish pastoral council officers, and parish finance council officers who took time out of their busy schedules to complete our surveys.

This book is dedicated to the parishioners, priests, and religious who carry out their stewardship and leadership roles by giving of their time and talent to serve on parish advisory councils.

Chapter One

Introduction to the Study of Consultative Councils

The ultimate basis for diocesan pastoral councils is not some political or managerial theory; as for any consultative body in the Church, the basis is theological, in keeping with the nature of the Church itself. The Church is the people of God built up by the Holy Spirit into a communion of believers, at once local and universal. Within that communion, certain principles based on the Church's own reality guide the working together of pastors and the rest of the people to form a more effective light to the nations. (Provost, 1999)

Consultative Councils in Catholic Parishes: Background from Vatican Documents

The Second Vatican Council made a strong case that consultative bodies in the Church are integral to its proper functioning. Such councils are an obvious expression of the Church as the people of God. The documents produced in the Second Vatican Council recognize that by virtue of their baptism, all the members of the faithful participate in the threefold ministry of Christ and the Church: as priest, prophet, and king — that is, to sanctify, teach, and govern "in accord with the condition proper to each One." In the Dogmatic Constitution on the Church (*Lumen Gentium*), the Council fathers argue that there is a fundamental equality of being equally called to holiness and discipleship that takes precedence over hierarchy.

Like all Christians, the laity have the right to receive in abundance the help of the spiritual goods of the Church, especially that of the word of God and the sacraments from the pastors. To the latter the laity should disclose their needs and desires with that liberty and confidence which befits children of God and brothers of Christ. By reason of the knowledge, competence or pre-eminence which they have the laity are empowered — indeed sometimes obliged — to manifest their opinion on those things which pertain to the good of the Church. If the occasion should arise this should be done through the institutions established by the Church for that purpose and always with truth, courage and prudence and with reverence and charity towards those who, by reason of their office, represent the person of Christ....

Many benefits for the Church are to be expected from this familiar relationship between the laity and the pastors. The sense of their own responsibility is strengthened in the laity, their zeal is encouraged, they are more ready to unite their energies to the work of their pastors. The latter, helped by the experience of the laity, are in a position to judge more clearly and more appropriately in spiritual as well as in temporal matters. Strengthened by all her members, the Church can thus more effectively fulfill her mission for the life of the world. (LG, 37)

As originally envisioned in the Decree on the Apostolate of the Laity (*Apostolicam Actuositatem*), councils were intended to assist the apostolic work of the Church either in the field of evangelization and sanctification or in the charitable, social, or other spheres.

...The parish offers an outstanding example of community apostolate, for it gathers into a unity all the human diversities that are found there and inserts them into the universality of the Church. The laity should develop the habit of working in the parish in close union with their priests, of bringing before the ecclesial community their own problems, world problems, and questions regarding man's salvation, to examine them together and solve them by general discussion. According to their abilities the laity ought to cooperate in all the apostolic and missionary enterprises of their ecclesial family.

The laity will continuously cultivate the "feeling for the diocese," of which the parish is a kind of cell; they will be always ready on the invitation of their bishop to make their own contribution to diocesan undertakings. Indeed, they will not confine their cooperation within the limits of the parish or diocese, but will endeavor, in response to the needs of the towns and rural districts, to extend it to interparochial, interdiocesan, national and international spheres. This widening of horizons is all the more necessary in the present situation, in which the increasing frequency of population shifts, the development of active solidarity and the ease of communications no longer allow any one part of society to live in isolation. The laity will therefore have concern for the needs of the People of God scattered throughout the world. Especially will they make missionary works their own by providing them with material means and even with personal service. It is for Christians a duty and an honor to give God back a portion of the goods they have received from him. (AA, 10)

In dioceses, as far as possible, councils should be set up to assist the Church's apostolic work, whether in the field of evangelization and sanctification or in the fields of charity, social relations and the rest; the clergy and religious working with the laity in whatever way proves satisfactory. These councils can take care of the mutual coordinating of the various lay associations and undertakings, the autonomy and particular nature of each remaining untouched.

Such councils should be found too, if possible, at the parochial, inter-parochial, inter-diocesan levels, and also on the national and international plane. (AA, 26)

This last line is the only direct reference to parish (parochial) councils found in the documents of the Second Vatican Council, and is frequently cited as the foundational document from which all parish councils derive.

Others argue that the model of today's parish "pastoral" council is the Vatican II Decree on the Pastoral Office of Bishops *(Christus Dominus*, par. 27). The 1965 Decree called for the formation of "pastoral" councils to assist bishops in a threefold process, i.e., "to investigate and consider matters relating to pastoral activity and to formulate practical conclusions concerning them." In 1973, the Congregation for the Clergy recommended the establishment of these "pastoral" councils at the parish level. The Congregation's 1973 "Private" or "Circular" Letter to the bishops of the world (*Omnes Christifideles*), the only Vatican document devoted in its entirety to pastoral councils, explicitly extended the language about Diocesan Pastoral Councils to the Parish Pastoral Councils (PPC). The consistent threefold description of the "pastoral" council's task in later Vatican documents, and the application of the "pastoral" terminology in the "Circular Letter" to the PPC, suggests that PPCs foster pastoral activity in the same threefold way as pastoral councils in general. (Fischer, 2001)

According to Mark F. Fischer, author of *Pastoral Councils in Today's Catholic Parishes*, in addition to extending the idea of council to the parish, the Congregation's 1973 letter also began a shift from the Decree on the Apostolate of the Laity as the source of the idea of councils to the Decree on the Pastoral Office of Bishops (*Christus Dominus*). As a structure and a means toward desirable dialogue, the pastoral councils, first recommended in Vatican II's Decree on the Pastoral Office of Bishops, clarified the purpose for councils at the parish level. They were to investigate and weigh pastoral undertakings and to formulate practical conclusions regarding them.

In exercising his office of father and pastor the bishop should be with his people as one who serves, as a good shepherd who knows his sheep and whose sheep know him....

In order to be able to provide for the welfare of the faithful as their individual circumstances demand, he should try to keep himself informed of their needs in the social circumstances in which they live. To this end he should employ suitable methods, especially social research. He should be solicitous for all men whatever their age, condition, nationality, whether they are natives, visitors or foreign immigrants. In exercising his ministry he should ensure that the faithful are duly involved in Church affairs; he should recognize their right and duty to play their part in building up the Mystical Body of Christ.... (CD, 16)

... Among the cooperators of the bishop in the governing of the diocese are included the priests who constitute his senate or council, such as the cathedral chapter, the council of consultors, or other committees according to the circumstances and character of different localities. These councils, and especially the cathedral chapters, should be reorganized, as far as is necessary, to suit contemporary needs.

Priests and laymen who are attached to the diocesan curia should be mindful that they are collaborating in the pastoral work of the bishop. The diocesan curia should be so organized that it may be a useful medium for the bishop, not only for diocesan administration, but also for pastoral activity.

It is highly desirable that in every diocese a special pastoral council be established, presided over by the diocesan bishop himself, in which clergy, religious, and laity specially chosen for the purpose will participate. It will be the function of this council to investigate and consider matters relating to pastoral activity and to formulate practical conclusions concerning them. (CD, 27)

The desirability of having a diocesan pastoral council which, "under the authority of the Bishop," is intended to "investigate and consider matters relating to pastoral activity and to formulate practical conclusions" has been reinforced in the Directory for the Pastoral Ministry of Bishops in 2004. The idea of a parish council being a pastoral council that is a *consultative* organ in which the faithful, expressing their baptismal responsibility, can assist the parish priest, who presides at the council, by offering their advice on pastoral matters" was further developed in a 2002 document from the Congregation for the Clergy, entitled *The Priest, Pastor and Leader of the Parish Community*.

In the general direction established in both the decree on the Apostolate of Lay People (*Apostolicam Actuositatem*), and the Decree on the Pastoral Office of Bishops (*Christus Dominus*) parish consultative bodies entered the law of the Church in 1983 with the publication of the new *Code of Canon Law*. After establishing the rights and responsibilities of the Christian faithful, the *Code* made specific reference to four consultative bodies on which lay faithful should serve in Canons 495-496, 511-514, 536, and 537. The diocesan pastoral council and the parish pastoral council are recommended in the *Code* "to the extent that pastoral circumstances recommend it" and if the bishop "judges it opportune." The pastoral council "is an expression of and instrument for lay coresponsibility and collaboration stemming from the Second Vatican Council realization that a parish is a community of the Christian faithful — a very basic, but relatively recently articulated reality focused on the pastoral care in the parish." (Coriden, 2008).

The diocesan finance council and the parish finance council were mandated in the 1983 *Code of Canon Law*, as a specific application of the general canonical rule (stated in Canon 1280) that every juridic person must have a finance council. Interestingly, it was the finance council that was added to the canons later in the *Code* revision process, after the provision for pastoral councils was already included. According to John Lynch, the provision of

Canon 537 was added after the 1977 draft, in the 1980 draft, apparently in response to replies from the circulation of the earlier one urging its inclusion (Lynch, 1982).

Consultative Councils in Catholic Parishes: Background from Canon Law

The Obligations and Rights of All the Christian Faithful

Canon 208. In virtue of their rebirth (Baptism) in Christ there exists among all the Christian faithful a true equality with regard to dignity and the activity whereby all cooperate in the building up of the Body of Christ in accord with each one's own condition and function.

Canon 212 §l. The Christian faithful, conscious of their own responsibility are bound by Christian obedience to follow what the sacred pastors, as representatives of Christ, declare as teachers of the faith or determine as leaders of the Church. §2. The Christian faithful are free to make known their needs, especially spiritual ones, and their desires to the pastors of the church. §3. In accord with the knowledge, competence and preeminence which they possess, they have the right and even at times a duty to manifest to the sacred pastors their opinion on matters which pertain to the good of the Church, and they have a right to make their opinion known to the other Christian faithful, with due regard for the integrity of faith and morals and reverence toward their pastors, and with consideration for the common good and the dignity of persons.

The Finance Council and the Finance Officer

Canon 492. In each diocese a finance council is to be established by the bishop over which he himself or his delegate presides and which is to be composed of at least three members of the Christian faithful truly skilled in financial affairs as well as in civil law, of outstanding integrity and appointed by the bishop.

The Pastoral Council

Canon 511. In each diocese, to the extent that pastoral circumstances recommend it, a pastoral council is to be established whose responsibility it is to investigate under the authority of the bishop all those things which pertain to pastoral works, to ponder them and to propose practical conclusions about them.

Parishes, Pastors, and Parochial Vicars

Canon 536 §1. After the diocesan bishop has listened to the presbyteral council and if he judges it opportune, a pastoral council is to be established in each parish; the pastor presides over it, and through it the Christian faithful along with those who share in the pastoral care of the parish in virtue of their office give their help in fostering pastoral activity. §2. This pastoral council possesses a consultative vote only and is governed by norms determined by the diocesan bishop.

Canon 537. Each parish is to have a finance council which is regulated by universal law as well as by norms issued by the diocesan bishop; in this council the Christian faithful, selected according to the same norms, aid the pastor in the administration of parish goods with due regard for the prescription of Canon 532.

Given the Canon Law requirement that all dioceses and parishes have finance councils, research to determine to what extent the law has been followed would be inhibited by the desire on the part of respondents to report conformity with the law. In any event, we were unable to identify any research that attempted to determine the degree of compliance with Canons 492 and 537.

In a survey of diocesan and eparchial bishops, conducted by the U.S. Conference of Catholic Bishops in 2003, it was reported that (consistent with Canon 511) more than half of the dioceses and eparchies have established diocesan pastoral councils (DPCs); several others are actively considering doing so (USCCB, 2004). In locations where DPCs are not currently active, some respondents reported that prior attempts at such bodies had proven ineffective, were difficult to conduct given largely rural geographic areas that made travel a hardship, or had temporarily lapsed due to a change in episcopal leadership. In locations where DPCs have been established, the bishops are directly involved in the work of the councils and believe DPCs provide fairly effective consultation and representative feedback that is of benefit in their episcopal leadership role.

This study also examined the degree to which diocesan bishops mandate or encourage parish pastoral councils, in a manner consistent with Canon 536. The study found that 65 percent of the respondents had mandated the establishment of parish pastoral councils in their diocese or eparchy and another 32 percent had encouraged parishes to establish them. They reported that an average of 85 percent of parishes had, in fact, established a parish pastoral council.

The Need for Effective Pastoral and Finance Councils in U.S. Parishes

Catholic parishes in the United States are being challenged by three major trends: demographic shifts, availability of clergy, and changing practices of Catholic people and expectations of their parish. The Catholic population is moving in three ways: 1) from concentrated areas of Catholics in cities to less concentrated and more religiously diverse areas in the suburbs; 2) from historically more Catholic areas of the Northeast and Upper Midwest to the sunbelt states of the Southeast and Southwest; and 3) from outside the United States to major U.S. urban centers and other areas in the Southeast and Southwest. The number of clergy available for parish ministry is declining while the average age of clergy is rising;

at the same time, the number of Catholics continues to increase. There are also differences in the practices and expectations of parish life on the part of Catholic people who grew up before and after the Second Vatican Council. Each of these trends puts pressure on the Church to expand or contract the number and type (clergy, religious, lay ecclesial worker) of staff, modify programs and ministries, and even restructure by establishing new parishes to address the needs of increasing numbers of parishioners or merging parishes where the number of parishioners, availability of clergy, or other resources can no longer sustain the parishes that are there.

Finally, revelations of clergy child sexual abuse in 2002 and settlement payments to victims by the Church have increased the call for more openness and transparency in decision-making in the Church. One of the important ways to provide information to parishioners and to obtain advice from them is through effectively functioning parish consultative structures that have already been established in the Church. In Pope John Paul II's apostolic exhortation delivered to a group of U.S. bishops shortly after the Synod of Bishops in 2003, he states:

> The Synod of Bishops acknowledged the need today for each Bishop to develop "a pastoral style which is ever more open to collaboration with all" (*Pastores Gregis*, 44), grounded in a clear understanding of the relationship between the ministerial priesthood and the common priesthood of the baptized (cf. *Lumen Gentium*,10). While the Bishop himself remains responsible for the authoritative decisions which he is called to make in the exercise of his pastoral governance, ecclesial communion also "presupposes the participation of every category of the faithful, inasmuch as they share responsibility for the good of the particular Church which they themselves form" (*Pastores Gregis*, loc. cit.). Within a sound ecclesiology of communion, a commitment to creating better structures of participation, consultation and shared responsibility should not be misunderstood as a concession to a secular

"democratic" model of governance, but as an *intrinsic requirement of the exercise of episcopal authority* and a necessary means of strengthening that authority. (Emphasis added by authors.)

Broad Goals of This Book

The "commitment to creating better structures of participation, consultation and shared responsibility ... as an intrinsic requirement of the exercise of episcopal authority and a necessary means of strengthening that authority" requires a knowledge of how the structures are currently working and a commitment to improve them. In addition, the Church literature reviewed in this chapter clearly identifies the threefold role of pastoral councils: under the pastor's direction, to investigate aspects of the parish ministry, to reflect on it, and to recommend conclusions. The intent of this book is to provide insight into not just the numbers and locations of these important consultative structure in parishes but also to consider how well they are functioning as groups and how well they are carrying out their mandates in the Church documents and Canon law, and in building communion among all the faithful in carrying out the mission of the Church.

In the remaining chapters, we will look at what is already known about parish pastoral and finance councils from the existing research (Chapter Two). We will then describe the approach used in this study to obtain a more complete profile of what is happening in the parish pastoral and finance councils in the United States today (Chapter Three).

We will look at the internal financial controls being reported by the parishes and the role of the finance council, in light of what is generally accepted as reasonable financial management practice in nonprofit organizations and what is called for in Church law (Chapter Four). We will also look at the extent to which parish advisory councils effectively communicate with the parish at large and with one another (Chapter Five).

We will then consider what the research on effective groups tells us and compare that literature to the parishes' descriptions of their councils, to discover if the councils are performing in ways that are consistent with what would be expected from effective groups (Chapter Six). Finally, we will identify some things that parishes and dioceses can do to ensure that parishes have effective pastoral and finance councils (Chapter Seven).

Chapter Two

What We Already Know about Parish Pastoral Councils and Parish Finance Councils

While relatively little research has been conducted on these two important parish advisory groups, there is some information available. This chapter summarizes the little that we do know about parish pastoral councils and parish finance councils. The chapter that follows presents summary statistics from our national survey of parish pastoral councils and parish finance councils. To begin, this chapter first examines the existing literature about parish pastoral councils and then parish finance councils.

What We Know about Parish Pastoral Councils

In spite of the fact that the concept of parish pastoral councils dates from Vatican II and that they became a fairly common phenomenon in the aftermath of the promulgation of the revised *Code of Canon Law* in 1983, we actually know relatively little about the practices of U.S. parish pastoral councils. What little we do know is the result of the work of a small group of scholars, a couple of polls, and a reading of the parish pastoral council guidelines disseminated by many U.S. dioceses.

The most notable scholar who has studied parish pastoral councils is Mark F. Fischer. In a series of articles that were published in *Today's Parish* magazine and that eventually culminated in his book *Pastoral Councils in Today's Catholic Parish*, Fischer examined virtually every aspect of the functioning of parish pastoral councils.

Fischer has suggested that the Council of Jerusalem (Galatians 2:1-10 and Acts 15:1-22) was actually the first pastoral council. The issue at hand was whether gentiles had to be circumcised in order to be granted full membership in the Church. Fischer likens it to a pastoral council meeting:

- Its subject was a pastoral matter with a focus on the Church's mission.
- The Council discussions involved passion, struggle, and new insights.
- Each participant brought their ministerial experience and commitment to the discussion.
- The discussion recognized the importance of Christian unity and communion with the larger Church.
- A practical conclusion was achieved through discernment and negotiation (Fischer, 1994b).

In both his articles and his book, Fischer examined parish pastoral councils on the basis of five dimensions: their purpose, their structure, their consultative function, their leadership, and the selection of their members. Taking Fischer's work as our starting point, and with due regard to the contributions of a handful of other scholars, this chapter examines the functioning of parish pastoral councils on the following dimensions:

1. Purpose and Functions
2. Organizational Structure
3. Membership
4. Meeting Procedures
5. Decision-Making Processes

As mentioned previously, we know little about parish pastoral council activities in each of these areas. What we do know comes from three very different sources. One is a reading of parish pastoral council guidelines issued by many dioceses. For the purpose of this study, a content analysis was performed on the parish pastoral council guidelines of 24 U.S. Catholic dioceses. These guidelines were downloaded from the various diocesan websites. A second source of information comes from a December 2003 survey conducted by the Committee on the Laity of the U.S. Conference of Catholic Bishops. They surveyed diocesan ordinaries to learn about their expectations for parish pastoral councils in their dioceses. Of the 195 surveys that were distributed to U.S. diocesan and eparchial bishops, 112 were returned (57 percent return rate). Naturally, to the extent that actual parish practices differ from the bishops' expectations, the results of this survey cannot provide us with the specifics that are available from the surveys supporting this current study. But the 2003 survey does provide some useful insights concerning the direction in which we might expect parish pastoral councils to be moving.

A third source of information comes from the results of the only known national survey of parish pastoral council members prior to this study's survey. It was conducted by the national organization Voice of the Faithful (VOTF) in spring 2004, and a summary was presented at the 2004 meeting of the Catholic Theological Society of America (Pohlhaus, 2004). While well-intentioned, the survey had one major operational drawback. It did not represent a random sample of parish pastoral councils. Rather, the survey was posted on-line and VOTF members were invited to complete it. A total of 1,064 VOTF members took advantage of this opportunity, but again, they do not represent a random sample. At best, this survey's results can be described as based on a sample of convenience. Nevertheless, it does provide some interesting background information.

Both surveys reveal that parish pastoral councils are taking hold. The USCCB survey found that 65 percent of the diocesan or eparchial respondents had mandated the establishment of parish pastoral councils in their diocese or eparchy and another 32 percent had encouraged parishes to establish them. They report that an average of 85 percent of parishes had in fact established a parish pastoral council. In 43 percent of the responding dioceses or eparchies, an office or staff person's sole responsibility was to offer support to parish pastoral councils.

The VOTF survey found that 93 percent of the respondents' parishes had parish pastoral councils in place. The average length of time that the parish pastoral councils in their sample had been in existence was 16 years.

With this background in place, we will now proceed to discuss each of the dimensions of parish pastoral councils.

The Five Dimensions of Parish Pastoral Councils

Parish Pastoral Council Purpose and Functions

There are two schools of thought as to the most important purpose and function of parish pastoral councils. Some argue that their primary purpose is pastoral planning, while others suggest that their primary purpose is to oversee and coordinate the activities of parish committees.

The leading proponent of parish pastoral councils as pastoral planners is Mark F. Fischer (2001). He argues that the parish pastoral council's main task is to articulate the parish's mission, identify goals flowing from that mission, and then define the objectives for reaching those goals. Actual implementation of the plan is the job of the pastor and parish staff. One good reason why the parish pastoral council should not be concerned with implementation issues, Fischer suggests, is because one of their functions is to evaluate the implementation. There would be a clear conflict of interest if they were responsible for both implementation of the pastoral plan and its evaluation.

In order to accomplish its planning function, according to Fischer, a parish pastoral council focuses on broad parish issues. It devotes most of its time to investigation and reflection on pastoral matters and then making recommendations to the pastor (i.e., the threefold role of the "pastoral" council as defined in the 1965 Decree on Bishops). While it may be assisted in its planning function by a committee structure, its scope exceeds that of merely overseeing committees. In fact, Fischer much prefers **parish** committees, not parish pastoral council committees. The implication is that parish committees report to the pastor. When a pastor accepts a parish pastoral council recommendation, he can then assign the implementation of that recommendation to the appropriate parish committee, to be carried out under his direction.

An alternative vision of a parish pastoral council is that of a council of ministries. This approach is typically associated with the work of the noted parish consultants Fr. Thomas Sweetser, SJ, and Carol Holden (Sweetser and Holden, 1987). It entails a parish pastoral council comprised of representatives of the various parish commissions. Typical parish commissions include those responsible for worship and spiritual life, education, community building, outreach, and administration. Each commission coordinates the activities and projects associated with its specific area of ministry. Each commission nominates members to serve on the parish pastoral council, which is then responsible for coordinating the activities of the commissions.

The appeal of the council of ministries approach is based on a number of factors (Fischer, 1995a). It decentralizes parish decision-making by distributing it across the parish commissions. In the process it empowers the lay leaders of the commissions, and thus is consistent with the principle of subsidiarity. The role that the pastoral council plays in coordinating commission activities prevents disorganization and overlap of activities. It gives the commissions freedom to operate but also ensures that they stay connected.

While the council of ministries emphasizes the importance of lay involvement, the pastoral planning council is more focused on carrying out the vision of the parish as found in its mission statement. Given these two competing approaches, what has been the experience?

Turning first to the 24 diocesan guidelines that we examined for this study, we found that the most frequently mentioned function of parish pastoral councils was around the theme of "setting the vision for the parish," which was included in 19 diocesan guidelines. That was followed closely by the themes of "planning for pastoral needs" and "recommending action to the pastor," each of which appeared in 15 diocesan guidelines. Responses associated with a council of ministries were found in only a few guidelines. For example, the themes of "coordinate parish activities and events" and "evaluate parish programs" were each found in only 5 diocesan guidelines.

The USCCB survey of bishops uncovered significantly different results. It found that while 95 percent of responding bishops suggest that their parish pastoral councils engage in pastoral planning, 64 percent of respondents nevertheless expect their councils to coordinate or oversee parish activities and 44 percent expect them to implement parish activities. There is an apparent discrepancy between what diocesan guidelines are telling parish pastoral councils and what their bishops expect of them.

The VOTF survey found that 65 percent of the respondents' parish pastoral councils listed planning as one of their functions while 48 percent listed "coordinate parish activities."

It appears that in practice, the expectation by both the bishops and the parish pastoral councils themselves is that the councils are responsible for both planning and for coordinating/ implementing. This is a lot to ask of a group of volunteers who typically only meet once a month.

Organizational Structure

The organizational structure dimension of parish pastoral councils refers to issues such as whether the council has a constitution and bylaws, issues surrounding council leadership, and relationships with other parish organizations.

Constitution and Bylaws

In establishing their constitution and bylaws, parish pastoral councils need to be keenly aware that their function is consultative only. They are expected to work collaboratively with the pastor, but they do not have a veto power nor can they enact policy on their own.

Their value to their parish resides in the collective wisdom of their members to understand parish needs and to convey them to the pastor. They need to understand and respect the pastor's right to reject any of their recommendations.

A review of the 24 sets of diocesan guidelines reveals that only 9 discuss parish pastoral council constitutions or by-laws. Most of those guidelines are vague on the topic, not going much beyond stating the parish pastoral council should establish them and suggesting some items that might be covered. But the Archdiocese of Baltimore provides each parish with a 13-page "Pastoral Council Constitution and Bylaws" document that lays out the important issues for the parish pastoral council, ranging from its purpose, procedures for the election of members, and a list of its standing committees. Some dioceses require that each parish's pastoral council constitution be approved by the bishop.

The USCCB's Committee on the Laity did not address this issue in their survey. The VOTF survey found that only 55 percent of the respondents' parish pastoral councils had established bylaws.

Council Leadership

Just as the pastor is the leader of the parish, so too, he should be the leader of the parish pastoral council. Some dioceses formalize the notion of the pastor as leader of the parish pastoral council by mandating that the pastor serve as the council's chairman. Others allow for the laity to hold leadership positions on the council, such as council chair, while still making it clear that the pastor "presides" over the council. This is consistent with Canon 536, which notes that the pastor presides over the parish by nature of the fact that the parish has been entrusted to him by the bishop.

The pastor's role as presider could take many forms, ranging from taking sole authority over setting the agenda and then serving as council chair to a more passive stance of listening to and participating in council deliberations. At a minimum, the pastor needs to communicate his vision to the council and actively seek the council's wisdom in defining problems and exploring solutions (Fischer, 1995b).

In addition to the pastor, the laity might assume leadership roles within the council. This is especially true in dioceses where the pastor is not formally designated as the council chair. Lay leaders could serve as chair of the parish pastoral council, or, as in the case of many parishes, on the council's executive committee, which typically includes the pastor and other council officers such as chair, vice-chair, or council secretary.

In our content analysis of 24 diocesan parish pastoral guidelines, there were 14 documents that addressed the issue of council chair. Only three designated the pastor as council chair, while the other 11 allowed for a lay person to serve as council chair. In addition, 12 guidelines specified other council officer positions (such as an executive committee). One of these mandated that the pastor select the other council officers, while 6 required that the other officers be elected by the council members. Neither the USCCB Committee on the Laity survey nor the VOTF survey addressed this issue.

Relationship with Other Parish Organizations

Naturally, to the extent that a parish pastoral council is a council of ministries, it will have close ties to other parish organizations. However, even a planning council might have its own standing subcommittees. In any event, it is important that parish pastoral councils relate to a variety of other parish organizations.

The most important of these other parish organizations is the parish finance council. As we have seen, unlike parish pastoral councils, parish finance councils are established by Canon Law. Clearly there needs to be a relationship between the two. But should they be separate councils, or should the parish finance council be merely a subcommittee of the parish pastoral council?

The argument in favor of the finance council serving as a subcommittee of the parish pastoral council rests on two points. The first point is the view that pastoral concerns should rank above financial matters. Second, most pastoral councils have at least some elected members that represent the entire parish, while parish finance councils typically consist entirely of members appointed by the pastor (Fischer, 1994a). On the other hand, the finances of a parish are a technical matter that many parish pastoral council members would find beyond the scope of their expertise.

Fischer (2001) attempts to resolve this matter by referring to the two types of knowledge recognized by Aristotle in his *Nicomachean Ethics*. One type of knowledge is scientific knowledge, knowledge that is always and everywhere true. The other type of knowledge is practical wisdom, knowledge sought through means of dialogue. Clearly, parish pastoral councils are concerned with practical knowledge and parish finance councils deal with scientific knowledge. The two councils not only search for different kinds of knowledge, but they use different methods in their search. Parish pastoral councils are more inclined to consult with fellow parishioners, while members of parish finance councils are more likely to be influenced by less subjective professional standards.

Clearly, the two groups need to consult with one another and coordinate their work. This coordination could entail subordinating one council to the other or it might be accomplished by simply having members from each council sit as *ex officio*, nonvoting members of the other council.

Of the 24 diocesan parish pastoral council guidelines that we examined, 13 address the relationship between the pastoral council and the parish finance council. Seven of these stress the importance of the independence of the pastoral council and the finance council, without making any recommendations as to how they might interact. Three require a member of the parish finance council to sit as an *ex officio* member of the parish pastoral council. One allows a finance council member to be either *ex officio* or a voting member of the pastoral council; one allows the finance council to either serve as a subcommittee of the pastoral council or be represented on the pastoral council in an *ex officio* basis; and one specifies that the finance council must be viewed as a subcommittee of the parish pastoral council.

With regard to its relationship with other parish organizations, clearly the parish pastoral council has a communications responsibility, whether it is construed as a council of ministries or as a planning council. Frequent reports to keep the entire parish informed of the council's activities are important. More detailed communications with specific parish organizations may also be called for.

In addition, both councils of ministries and planning councils are called upon to perform evaluations. Councils of ministries evaluate how well the various parish commissions are carrying out their directives. Planning councils evaluate how well their plan is being implemented and how it can be improved upon. Both need to acquire feedback from parish organizations to carry out their evaluations.

In 14 of the diocesan guideline documents, the relationship between the parish pastoral council and other parish organizations is described. Nine of these envision a one-way street, with the pastoral council merely receiving reports from other parish organizations. Three dioceses expect their parish pastoral councils to set goals and priorities and to guide the work of these other organizations. Two dioceses go even further and call for parish organizations to submit goals and objectives to the parish pastoral council for approval.

Membership

Most parish pastoral councils contain a variety of different types of membership. Some members will have been elected, using one of the selection methods described below. Others will have been appointed by the pastor. Still others sit on the council by virtue of their position in the parish. For example, all parish clergy, including parochial vicars and deacons, typically are eligible to serve on the council. Likewise, provision might be made for the on-going membership of the parochial school principal or other key parish staff members. In the previous section, we saw that it is not uncommon for a representative from the parish finance council to sit on the parish pastoral council. No matter how they achieved their membership, it is important that council members understand their role, and that they are qualified to carry out that role.

Membership issues include matters of representation, member selection, and terms of office.

Representation

One of the goals of many dioceses and parishes is to ensure that their parish pastoral council is "representative." This could go beyond merely ensuring that the council is diverse, reflecting the differences among parishioners. It might involve ensuring that every element of the parish is represented on its pastoral council: every ethnic group, parochial school parents, religious education parents, young adults, senior citizens, etc., so that the composition of the council mirrors the composition of the parish. Frequently a pastor will use his authority to appoint members to ensure that the parish pastoral council is indeed representative of the entire parish. But as Mark F. Fischer reminds us (Fischer, 1992b), just because an individual is representative of an important parish group, it does not necessarily follow that he or she will make an effective council member.

Of course, the danger in designing a parish pastoral council to be deliberately representative is not only that the council might not include the most qualified parishioners, but that members who are selected may feel that they represent a particular constituency and they should function as an advocate for that constituency. This could result in their basing their decision-making on what is best for their constituency and not necessarily what is best for the parish as a whole.

Selection

In addition to its appointed and *ex officio* members, parish pastoral councils typically are comprised of members who have been selected through some parishwide selection process. The two most common methods are a parishwide election and a process of discernment. Both councils of ministries and planning councils can employ either method.

A parishwide election is a familiar process. Candidates are nominated, either by their fellow parishioners or, as the case of a council of ministries, by the commissions that they represent. This might be followed by a period of vetting, where the candidates learn more about the responsibilities of a council member and decide if they wish to remain a candidate. Then the entire parish votes to elect the number of new council members that are needed in that particular year.

One of the risks of selecting parish pastoral council members through a parishwide vote is that parishioners in a large parish simply might not know enough about the candidates to cast an educated ballot and so the election might become a popularity contest.

An alternative to the popular vote method is a process known as discernment. This method relies on a dialogue among candidates and selectors and allows all parties to reflect on the qualities needed by the council and to scrutinize the extent to which each candidate possesses those qualities. Mark F. Fischer (2003) has identified four stages of discernment:

1. Sharing of information about the parish pastoral council
2. A series of open parish meetings where parishioners are nominated
3. A separate series of open parish meetings where parishioners examine each nominee in dialogue
4. Selection of the council members by those parishioners who had participated in the process

According to Fischer, this process serves to create interest in the parish pastoral council and to educate both parishioners and nominees on the issues that the council must consider. This process can be applied to both councils of ministries and planning councils. In the case of councils of ministries, the candidates have been nominated by their commissions, but otherwise the discernment process is as described above.

The trade-off between an election and discernment is that, on one level, discernment is a less inclusive process in that typically fewer parishioners will get involved than in a parishwide election. On the other hand, discernment is a more open process in that, through reflection and dialogue, both nominees and selectors are forced to clarify their vision of the council. This makes for a more educated selection process.

Of the 24 diocesan parish pastoral council guidelines that we analyzed, 21 address the issue of parish pastoral council membership selection. Most of these stress the importance of the council membership being representative of the entire parish community. A variety of selection methods are called for in 17 of the diocesan guidelines, including election, discernment, and appointment. Only 1 recommends that all council members be popularly elected after a nomination process. Another gives the pastor the authority to appoint all of the council members after consulting with parishioners. Still another relies on a "Discernment Committee" to select the council members once the first three stages of the discernment process described above have been completed. One diocese recommends that parish pastoral council members be chosen by lot among those who have been nominated after the parish community has prayed over the matter.

Terms

Most parish pastoral councils set terms, typically three years, for their members and stagger the terms so that not too many members turn over in any one year. Likewise, most set a limit on the number of consecutive terms that can be served.

The matter of terms for parish pastoral council members was contained in 13 of the 24 diocesan guidelines that we studied. The most frequent recommendation was for three year terms, with a maximum of two consecutive terms. This applies to both selected and appointed members. One diocese offers the opportunity for the entire council to turn over at the same time, rather than staggering the selection, so that a whole new council is in place every three years.

Meeting Procedures

Like any other similar organization, parish pastoral councils need a set of procedures under which they will conduct their meetings. This could mean invoking *Robert's Rules of Order*, or it might be very informal. Whatever the parish chooses to do, the procedures should be agreed upon in advance and codified, most likely in the council's constitution and bylaws.

Among the items that need to addressed are who sets the agenda, typical agenda items, how often will the council meet, and to what extent will council meetings be open to non-council members.

Agenda Setting

There is an old axiom that states, "He who controls the agenda controls the meeting." An important measure of control is the ability to determine what items are included on the agenda to be addressed by the parish pastoral council and, just as important, what items *do not* make the agenda and therefore do not merit council consideration. A primary issue here is the extent to which the pastor should maintain control over the agenda.

One argument is that by opening up the agenda setting and sharing (or even delegating) that responsibility with other members of the council, the pastor is displaying confidence in the other members and helping to foster leadership among them. The counterargument is that to the extent that the pastor abdicates this responsibility, the parish pastoral council might spend time on issues that the pastor thinks are unimportant or even move in a direction contrary to the pastor's vision for the parish. Keep in mind, the parish pastoral council is a consultative body to the pastor, who is responsible for making final decisions.

A separate, but related, issue concerns whether or not parishioners who are not members of the parish pastoral council should have the opportunity to submit agenda items to the council. Providing parishioners with the opportunity to submit agenda items is certainly a powerful mechanism for keeping them interested in the work of the council and for providing them with an incentive to buy into decisions emanating from the council. At the same time, it needs to be emphasized to them that there are many potential issues that the council needs to consider, and that there is a good chance that their agenda suggestion might not make the final agenda. Again, the danger is that parishioners' agenda recommendations might involve issues of low priority or might steer the parish in a direction other than that envisioned by the pastor.

If parishioners are allowed to submit agenda items, it is crucial that they be notified of the disposition of their agenda item. If it is not selected to be included on the agenda, the parishioner should be so informed, with a brief explanation. If it is included, the parishioner should be notified, along with the disposition of the item. The parish pastoral council might even choose to invite the agenda submitter to attend the meeting where the item is discussed as an observer (see below).

In any event, allowing individuals to submit agenda items is one thing. Deciding what items are actually included in the final meeting agenda is of even greater importance. We can envision a very open agenda-submitting process, accompanied by a rather closed agenda-determining process.

Our analysis of diocesan guidelines for parish pastoral councils reveals that 11 of the 24 dioceses included a discussion of the agenda submission issue. Most allow for multiple actors to submit agenda items: primarily the pastor and other members of the council. A few allow agenda submissions from parish staff members who were not part of the parish pastoral council. Four diocesan guidelines permit agenda submissions from parishioners who were not council members. Most of the guidelines that deal with agenda setting indicate that this task is the responsibility of the council's executive committee, of which the pastor is a member.

The USCCB's Committee on the Laity survey did not address the issue of agenda setting. The VOTF survey found that in 72 percent of the respondents' parishes, parish pastoral council members have the right to submit agenda items. In 62 percent of these parishes, parishioners who are not members of the council have this ability. In 60 percent of these parishes, the pastor retains primary responsibility for determining the final agenda from among the items that had been submitted.

Typical Agenda Items

Regardless of the specific topics to be discussed, almost all observers agree that each meeting should start with a prayer (Turley,

1995), include some time for faith sharing, and conclude with a meeting evaluation (Rogers, 1995).

In discussing the prayer component of a parish pastoral council meeting, Turley makes the point that a substantial amount of time should be devoted to prayer. She argues that the prayer should not be merely "bookend prayer" that opens and closes a meeting, but should attempt to genuinely move council members' hearts and change lives. On a similar theme, Rogers suggests a theological basis for meeting evaluation, citing *Exodus* 7:17, "Is the Lord among us or not" as a possible theme of the evaluation. An honest evaluation should be viewed as an act of love. She recommends that both content and process be evaluated and suggests the use of both formal and informal evaluations.

The evaluation of diocesan guidelines for parish pastoral councils found that 12 of the 24 dioceses studied recommended agenda items to their parishes. Eight of these mentioned prayer, three mentioned both prayer and formation activity, and one listed only faith formation. None mentioned meeting evaluation.

The survey of bishops conducted by the USCCB Committee on the Laity found that 71 percent recommend that prayer and faith sharing be regular agenda items for their parish pastoral councils. These issues were not included in the VOTF survey.

Frequency of Meeting

There is no correct answer as to how often a parish pastoral council should meet. It depends entirely on the individual parish's situation. Frequency of meetings is covered in 12 of the 24 diocesan parish pastoral guidelines that we examined. Most of these recommend monthly meetings while requiring a minimum number (e.g., quarterly) of meetings.

The USCCB's Committee on the Laity survey did not ask about meeting frequency. The VOTF survey indicated that 69 percent of the respondents' parish pastoral councils met monthly, and another 9 percent met bi-monthly. Less than 1 percent met annually.

Open Meetings

Like the issue of agenda submissions, the issue of whether parish pastoral council meetings should be open to the entire parish can be a controversial one. Those who advocate open meetings base their support on essentially the same arguments that we saw above for open agenda submissions: allowing parishioners to attend meetings as observers will heighten their interest in the work of the council and provide them with an incentive to buy into decisions emanating from the council. The counterargument is that the parish pastoral council is a deliberative body that needs to allow its members to "think out loud" in the process of their discussions without fear of their statements leaving the room. Having outside observers could stifle the quality of the deliberative process.

Of the 24 diocesan guidelines for parish pastoral councils that we examined, only 6 make provisions for open meetings. They do so without exception. One even allows for non-council members to be provided with the opportunity to speak at council meetings with prior approval of the council's executive committee.

The issue of open meetings was not included in the survey distributed by the USCCB's Committee on the Laity. The VOTF survey revealed that 68 percent of the respondents' parish pastoral councils had made provision for open meetings.

Decision-Making Processes

Related to the issue of parish pastoral council meeting procedures are the issues of how the council will arrive at its recommendations and which matters are appropriate for council consideration.

Most observers recognize that, just as the Church is not a democracy, neither is a parish pastoral council. It is generally agreed that council recommendations should not be formed on the basis of majority vote. Rather, the council should be engaged in a discernment process (not unlike that mentioned above) and strive to reach a consensus. As Dennis O'Leary (1995) reminds us, consensus does not mean unanimity of agreement, but rather substantial commitment to a particular direction. It does not involve a majority vote nor does it require some members to simply "give in" in order to move forward. If a consensus cannot be reached, it is wise to table the matter (if practical) and place it on the agenda for a future meeting. This allows council members to reconsider their positions or even to generate some alternative approaches to addressing the issue.

As has been mentioned numerous times, the parish pastoral council is a consultative body. This implies an honest effort on the part of both the pastor and the council to engage in a meaningful dialogue. The pastor is free to accept its recommendations or reject them. However, not every parish-related issue is appropriate for council consideration. The pastor needs to decide the types of issues for which he values council input and the types for which he believes consultation with the council is not appropriate or would not be helpful.

Mark F. Fischer (1992a) lays out some rules of thumb for determining which issues are appropriate for parish pastoral council consideration. In general, Fischer notes that matters that require technical judgments are not suitable for a group of generalists like a parish pastoral council. On the other hand, issues affecting the entire parish community, and which can be informed by experienced community members (such as council members), are most fitting for consideration by the council.

According to Fischer, matters should be brought before the parish pastoral council and a consensus sought only when *all* of the following are in place:

1. the technical accuracy of the decision is not crucial, and
2. the issue is so unstructured that no single individual would be expected to have a comprehensive understanding of it, and
3. the acceptance of the decision by the entire council is crucial.

Pastoral matters that fail one or more of these tests might still be brought before the council for its wisdom, but without the necessity of attempting to secure a consensus.

Fourteen of the 24 diocesan guidelines for parish pastoral councils consider the issue of council decision-making. None of them recommend that decisions be reached by majority vote. All of them recommend some combination of discernment and/or consensus. The survey conducted by the USCCB Committee on the Laity did not ask about parish pastoral council decision-making processes. The VOTF survey discovered that respondents' councils employed a variety of decision-making techniques. Most (63 percent) reached their decision by consensus and 32 percent indicated that they employed a process of discernment. About a third made at least some decisions by voting, and 15 percent indicated that they did not reach decisions.

Other Parish Pastoral Council Issues

There are a variety of other parish pastoral issues which could be assigned to one of our five dimensions, but about which we know little or nothing. These include matters such as the extent to which education or training is provided to council members, methods used to communicate council activities to parishioners, and the effectiveness of the council's internal group processes. None of these have been extensively studied, but they were addressed in our survey and are discussed in later chapters.

There is one other topic that needs to be considered before we move on to the next section. Due to a variety of causes, including the current priest shortage, many priests have been called upon to serve as pastor of more than one parish, a situation that is known by a variety of terms, such as "clustering" or "twinning." Some dioceses have found that clusterwide pastoral councils, known as "inter-parochial pastoral councils," are useful in serving these clustered parishes, just as parish pastoral councils are useful for individual parishes.

Most of what is known about inter-parochial pastoral councils is contained in a study conducted by Robert Miller (2007) as part of the Lilly Endowment funded "Emerging Models of Pastoral Leadership" project. In an exploratory qualitative study intended to investigate the development of multiparish pastoral councils among Catholic parishes, the author describes the pastors' perspectives on multiparish pastoral councils based on telephone interviews with pastors. This study suggests that these councils are being employed in a variety of creative ways but that pastors frequently need to adapt policy and procedures designed for individual parish pastoral councils to create the methods that they use in their multiparish councils.

The vision of the pastor clearly determines the nature of the purpose for a multiparish pastoral council and the way it is formed and operates. If the pastor is concerned about securing the separate identity of his parishes and/or if geography or other circumstances make it unlikely that the parishes involved would ever be able to share much other than their pastor, the chosen model is most typically **Type A — Parallel,** in which individual parish pastoral councils meet simultaneously or sequentially with the pastor present at each. The work of these individual parish councils might need to be augmented by a **Type B — Additional,** multiparish council that would advise the pastor on a very limited agenda of coordinating only those areas necessary, such as the funding of the pastor's position and the Mass schedule.

If, after an assessment of the geographical arrangement and the resources and needs of the parishes, the pastor envisions the parishes involved as eventually benefiting by sharing a wide range of resources — even to the point where the parishes might merge sometime in the future, representatives from each of the parishes are formed into a **Type C — Replacement** pastoral council instead of individual parish pastoral councils. This model involves parishioners from different parishes coming to know and understand one another and to form the plan of an integrated ministry among the existing parishes or a future new parish.

Because of the presumption of the "one pastor, one parish" model in Canon law, there is little provision for alternate models for consultation of the laity. Canon 537 calls for each parish to have a finance council which is regulated by universal law as well as by norms issued by the diocesan bishop. However, there is some evidence from the field that this is sometimes ignored in practice. Some pastors of multiple parishes have a single finance council that consults for all the parishes administered by him. In at least one known instance, the pastor meets with one finance and pastoral council as a single consultative body for three parishes.

For pastoral councils there is more flexibility built into the law, since the diocesan bishop alone develops the norms and guidelines under which pastoral councils operate. However, there is little evidence that diocesan policy has been developed to govern the range of possibilities for multiple parish councils. In the absence of diocesan policy, pastors are employing councils in multiparish settings by adapting what is known about a single parish council to a council or councils with much greater complexity.

What We Know about
Parish Finance Councils

As little as we know about parish pastoral councils, we know even less about parish finance councils. No scholar of the stature of Mark F. Fischer has made understanding finance councils their academic pursuit. There have been no national surveys of bishops or parish finance council members to learn about council activities.

On the other hand, as was pointed out in Chapter One, unlike parish pastoral councils, parish finance councils are grounded in Canon Law — so there has been some discussion of the Canon Law implications. Also, most dioceses have put into place guidelines for parish finance councils and the internal financial controls of parishes, which the parish finance councils oversee. While we do not have pre-existing survey information on parish finance councils, we do have diocesan guidelines to provide us with information. As with parish pastoral councils, individual parishes might not always abide by diocesan guidelines, but at a minimum these guidelines offer a glimpse of the direction that parish finance councils are likely to be taking. For the purposes of this study, we conducted a content analysis on 29 diocesan parish finance council guidelines taken from diocesan websites. Of these, 22 were different dioceses than those used for the content analysis of parish pastoral council guidelines. Only 7 dioceses appeared in both samples. This section considers three dimensions of parish finance councils:

1. Membership
2. Meetings
3. Responsibilities

Dimensions of Parish Finance Councils

Membership

Unlike parish pastoral councils, members of parish finance councils are almost always appointed by the pastor. Referencing Mark F. Fischer's (2001) dichotomy of knowledge, parish finance council members are expected to have scientific knowledge, not practical wisdom as Aristotle has defined the terms. They need to understand Generally Accepted Accounting Principles, including those that apply to nonprofit organizations, investment strategies, insurance, and a whole host of other technical financial issues. Obviously, the selection of members cannot be left up to a popular vote or even a discernment process.

Diocesan guidelines for parish finance councils recognize the importance of appointing, rather than electing, parish finance council members, although a handful did recommend that the parish finance council, like the parish pastoral council, be representative of the entire parish. Of the 29 diocesan guidelines studied, 20 covered the matter of membership selection. All but 1 gave the pastor final say on the appointment of parish finance council members, often after conferring with the current finance council or the parish pastoral council. The guidelines of one diocese allow for parish finance membership selection to be determined either by a parishwide nomination followed by a popular vote, or by the nomination of parishioners from a nominating committee, with selection drawn by lot. Under either method, candidates need to be approved by the pastor.

Diocesan guidelines for the number of members of a parish finance council vary considerably, ranging from 2 to 12. Most recommend a range of 3 to 7. A handful observes that parish finance council members must be free of any conflicts of interest. Concerning the length of the terms of appointment, all 19 guidelines that address the issue recommend that a term should exceed two years. Continuity among the parish finance council membership, since it involves technical matters, is possibly even more important than continuity among parish pastoral council membership. Most guidelines permit members to serve for more than one term.

Meetings

The two primary issues concerned with the meetings dimension are those of the frequency and establishing who serves as the parish finance council chair. Twenty-four of the 29 diocesan guidelines for parish finance councils specified a minimum number of meetings. At least quarterly meetings were recommended in 19 dioceses, 4 recommended monthly meetings, and 1 diocese indicated that meetings should be held at least semiannually.

A more important issue is the matter of who serves as the parish finance council chair and thus conducts the meeting. Our analysis found that 13 dioceses address that issue. Five indicate that the pastor should serve as chair; 4 recommend that the pastor appoint a member other than himself to serve as chair; and 4 recommend that the finance council elect its own chair.

Responsibilities

We can divide the responsibilities that parish finance councils could conceivably take on into three types: tasks concerned with the evaluation and review of parish financial statements, parish managerial decision-making extending beyond these tasks, and overseeing internal parish financial controls. Since Chapter Four is entirely devoted to the topic of parish internal financial controls, we only consider the first two of these responsibilities here.

Evaluation and Review of Parish Financial Statements

The content analysis of the 29 diocesan parish finance guidelines reveals that 17 mention responsibilities in the area of the evaluation and review of parish financial statements explicitly. Of course, one might argue that these responsibilities exist implicitly in the Canon Law description of parish finance councils.

The most frequently mentioned finance council responsibility is to review and evaluate the parish balance sheet (found in 16 diocesan guidelines). The next most frequently mentioned responsibility is to evaluate the amount of cash on hand (mentioned in 8 diocesan guidelines). Comparing actual spending and revenues to budgeted amounts and reviewing the amount of debt outstanding were responsibilities listed in 7 guidelines. Surprisingly, only 1 diocese explicitly stated that the finance council should compare current budget figures to those of the prior year. Again, many of these responsibilities are implicit in the nature of a parish finance council.

Parish Managerial Decision-Making

Perhaps more revealing are the other tasks that some dioceses assign to the parish finance council. In addition to the obvious one of approving (and in some cases developing) the parish operating budget, which was mentioned in 26 diocesan guidelines, 13 dioceses make the finance council responsible for long-term parish financial and physical needs. Eight dioceses involve the parish finance council in the hiring and firing of senior parish staff. Seven dioceses give the finance council responsibility for the parish's financial policy. Only 3 dioceses anticipate that the finance council would be involved in contracting with outside vendors.

Summary

We actually know surprisingly little about the activities of either parish pastoral councils or parish finance councils. Until now, good data have not been available. This study begins to fill that void by providing data on the activities of the first scientifically drawn national sample of parish advisory councils. Survey results are presented in succeeding chapters, starting with Chapter Three in which we present some basic statistics that provide information on the five dimensions of parish pastoral councils and the three dimensions of parish finance councils for the parishes in our sample.

Chapter Three

Methodology of the Study and Descriptive Information about Parish Pastoral Councils and Parish Finance Councils

Background of the Study

In 2006, the authors established collaboration between the Center for the Study of Church Management (CSCM) at Villanova University, the Center for Applied Research in the Apostolate (CARA) at Georgetown University, and Robert J. Miller, director of the Office of Research and Planning of the Archdiocese of Philadelphia to conduct this study of consultative bodies in U.S. parishes. CSCM assumed primary responsibility in procuring funding for the project and handled all mailing, follow-up, and data entry.

The four authors developed a set of questionnaires to elicit information about the composition, structure, and operation of parish pastoral councils and parish finance councils in parishes that have such consultative bodies. The questionnaires were designed to be as similar in format as possible, with parallel questions about each consultative body whenever possible. Overlapping questions about more general parish characteristics were combined into a single-informant questionnaire to be completed by the pastor or another parish staff member. CARA then drew a random sample of 3,076 parishes from its National Parish Inventory (NPI), a national database of parish life that was compiled by CARA in 1999 and has been updated periodically since that time.

In winter 2007, three separate surveys were sent to each parish — a single-informant questionnaire on parish characteristics, a questionnaire for the parish council president, and a questionnaire for the parish finance council president. Each of the question-naires was marked with a unique parish code so that they could be identified by parish even if they were not all mailed back together. A total of 149 surveys were undeliverable, most typically because the parish no longer existed. After multiple follow-ups, 661 parishes returned at least one of the surveys, for a response rate of 22.5 percent. Parishes returned 537 parish council questionnaires (18.5 percent) and 530 parish finance council questionnaires (18.1 percent). Among parishes that completed a parish council questionnaire, 95 percent also completed the questionnaire on parish characteristics.

Description of the Parishes in This Sample

In this section, we describe the characteristics of parishes that responded to the surveys and then compare those parishes to the typical characteristics of other parishes nationally that we have learned from CARA's National Parish Inventory.

Responding parishes tend to be a little larger than the typical parish. On average, these parishes have a little over 1,000 registered households, compared to 855 registered households in the typical U.S. parish, according to NPI. Their average year of founding was 1912 and their average approximate annual budget is just under $700,000.

These parishes also tend to have more staff than the typical parish — they average 5 full-time parish staff (working 30 or more hours per week in the parish) and 4 part-time parish staff. By comparison, the NPI reports that parishes nationally average 4.6 parish staff (both full-time and part-time).

On average, these responding parishes have had the same leader for the last seven years. In two-thirds of the parishes, the pastor is responsible for only that parish, but one in three reports that the pastor administers more than one parish.

Clustering, or linking several parishes administratively, is an approach that many bishops are employing to respond to the declining number of priests available to pastor parishes. In these "cluster parishes," two or more nearby parishes are assigned — usually to just one priest, but sometimes more than one — to pastor and administer. Each parish remains open and territorially distinct, but they are administered by a single priest who is pastor of both parishes and coordinates the Mass schedule so that he can preside at liturgy and be available at each parish in turn. Just over a third of the parishes in this survey (34 percent) are clustered or linked with another parish — on average, they are clustered or linked with two other parishes.

Just 4 percent of responding parishes are entrusted to some–one other than a priest, under Canon 517§2. This is a special provision, included in the 1983 revised *Code of Canon Law*, which is used by bishops to provide pastoral care for a parish when there is no priest available to be assigned.

The parishes in this survey represent parishes from all different urban and rural areas. About 40 percent of the responding parishes are located in a small town or a rural area. Just over three in ten are in a large town (10,000 to 50,000 residents), a small city (50,000 to 100,000 residents), or the suburbs of a small city. The other 28 percent are in a city of more than 100,000 residents or its suburb.

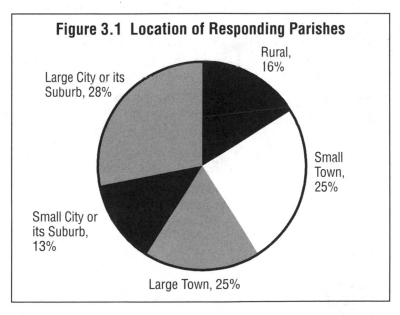

Figure 3.1 Location of Responding Parishes

Rural, 16%

Large City or its Suburb, 28%

Small Town, 25%

Small City or its Suburb, 13%

Large Town, 25%

Finally, more than nine in ten responding parishes report having a parish pastoral council (93 percent) or a parish finance council (93 percent). These percentages likely overestimate the actual proportion of parishes with such councils, in part because parishes with these consultative bodies are more likely to have completed and returned a survey. Particularly for parish pastoral councils (henceforth PPC), the actual percentage among all parishes is likely somewhat lower.[1]

While a parish finance council (henceforth PFC) is mandated in Canon Law, there is no corresponding mandate for parish pastoral councils. The *Code of Canon Law* (Canon 536§1) states that "If the diocesan bishop judges it opportune … a pastoral council is to be established in each parish." The research summarized by Mark F. Fischer, however, suggests that these consultative bodies are increasingly common among parishes. Citing research from 1970 to 1995, Fischer reports estimates of between 50 percent and 79 percent of all parishes with councils (Fischer, 2001).

Among parishes that report that they do not currently have a PPC, close to half report that the PPC is undergoing reorganization. On average, parishes report that their parish pastoral council has been in existence for 21 years. The average parish finance council has been in existence for 19 years. Parishes that report no PFC tend to report that they never had a PFC (47 percent) or that the PFC is undergoing reorganization (33 percent).

In this chapter, we discuss the findings from our surveys within the context of the Five Dimensions of Parish Pastoral Councils and the Three Dimensions of Parish Finance Councils as presented in Chapter Two.

Parish Pastoral Councils

Parish Pastoral Council Purpose and Function

In Chapter Two we saw that there are essentially two visions of the primary purpose and function of a parish pastoral council.

---

1. CARA's National Parish Inventory reported in 2000 that an estimated 82 percent of all parishes have a Parish Pastoral Council (Gautier and Perl, 2000).

One vision is that the council serves primarily as a planning group. The other vision assigns to the council the role of overseeing and coordinating parish groups. Naturally, many parish pastoral councils assume both roles. What kinds of functions do respondents believe were important and in which were they most involved? In Table 3.1 we see that, as might be expected of a consultative body, the largest proportion (65 percent) respond that it is "very important" that the PPC make recommendations to the pastor. This was also the function that the largest proportion (58 percent) believed the PPC was "very" involved in. But that doesn't answer the question as to the purpose of the council: both planning and coordinating councils would presumably be responsible for making recommendations to the pastor.

Table 3.1 shows that, among those responding, 63 percent of the PPCs believe that it is very important that the council set a vision for the parish; 51 percent of the councils indicate that they are very involved in this process. When asked specifically about parish pastoral planning, 56 percent of the PPCs indicate that it is very important that they engage in planning; 43 percent agree that they are in fact very involved in pastoral planning.

By way of comparison, 42 percent of the parish pastoral councils in our sample believe that it is very important that the council coordinate parish activities; 31 percent indicate that the council is very involved in coordinating parish activities. Similarly, 38 percent of the councils think that it is very important that the council facilitate communication among parish groups; 26 percent agree that the council is very involved in this activity.

Based on these figures, PPCs in our sample were more likely to view themselves as planning councils than as coordinating councils. In fact, those activities associated with the coordinating function were among those in which the PPCs indicated they were the least involved.

Other functions in which the PPCs in our sample were very involved include building community (50 percent) as well as serving as a sounding board for parishioners (50 percent) and the pastor and his staff (48 percent). As noted in Chapter Two, parish pastoral councils that take on multiple functions are asking a lot

Table 3.1 Parish Pastoral Council Functions

	Percentage Responding Important		Percentage Responding Involved	
	Somewhat	Very	Somewhat	Very
Coordinating Parish Activities	34%	42%	36%	31%
Developing Parish Community	32	58	34	50
Developing Parish Policy	30	54	39	41
Evaluating Parish Programs	32	41	41	28
Facilitating Communication	38	38	42	26
Planning for Pastoral Needs	30	56	39	43
Recommending Action to the Pastor	28	65	33	58
Serving as Parish Sounding Board for Pastor/Staff	28	57	33	48
Serving as Parish Sounding Board for Parishioners	30	58	32	50
Serving as Parish Sounding Board for Parish Groups	35	50	37	42
Setting Parish Vision	26	63	34	51
Studying Issues In-Depth	42	40	40	35

from a group of volunteers who might typically meet only once per month.

Structure of the Parish Pastoral Council

Parish pastoral councils are not formed in a vacuum. Nearly all of the parishes in our sample (87 percent) operate under written by-laws, such as governing principles, policies, or guidelines. Our recent search of diocesan websites reveals that at least 33 dioceses have written guidelines for parish pastoral councils published on their website. More than half (55 percent) of the parishes responding to the survey indicate that they are aware of norms for forming a parish pastoral council that are provided by the diocese.

A third of responding parishes report that they sponsor a parish-based program of education or formation for preparing pastoral council members to serve. Some dioceses offer an orientation program for parish pastoral councils, and 21 percent of responding parishes indicate that they are aware of such a program in the diocese. Other dioceses have a diocesan office with consulting support for parish pastoral councils, and 17 percent of responding parishes say that the diocese offers this support. Still other dioceses offer diocesan-sponsored retreats or other formation opportunities for parish pastoral councils — 15 percent of responding parishes are aware that their diocese offers these opportunities.

Meeting Chair and Officers

The parish pastoral council chairperson chairs the meeting in three out of four PPCs. In another 14 percent, however, it is the pastor who chairs the meetings. Another 11 percent of PPCs have some sort of shared arrangement, whereby both the PPC chairperson and the pastor collaborate to chair the PPC meetings.

As Table 3.2 shows, the pastor is a little more likely to chair the PPC in smaller parishes, in the Northeast or the West, in rural areas or in large cities, and in parishes where he is responsible for more than one parish. Interestingly, nearly all responding parishes that have a Parish Life Coordinator report that the PPC chairperson chairs the meeting. None of these parishes report a

Table 3.2 Person Who Chairs the PPC Meetings, by Selected Parish Characteristics

	Pastor/PLC	Chairperson	Both, in Collaboration	N
Parish Households				
Less than 300	17%	71%	12%	115
300 to 699	17	73	10	126
700 to 1,399	9	84	7	122
1,400 and over	12	76	12	124
Census Region				
Northeast	23%	68%	9%	155
Midwest	9	80	11	220
South	11	77	12	110
West	17	70	13	47
Location				
Large city (over 100,000)	21%	68%	11%	72
Suburb of large city	13	79	8	64
Small city or its suburb	15	76	9	61
Large town (10,000 to 50,000)	9	78	13	91
Small town (under 10,000)	10	81	9	128
Rural	21	67	12	81
Leadership				
Pastor of only this parish	13%	77%	10%	328
Pastor of multiple parishes	17	69	15	150
Parish Life Coordinator	8	92	0	24
Entire Sample	***14%***	***75%***	***11%***	***532***

shared arrangement such that both the PPC chairperson and the Parish Life Coordinator collaborate in chairing the meetings.[2]

In addition to the chair of the PPC, nearly three in four PPCs also have other officers. In most cases (80 percent) the other officers are elected by the PPC. However, about one in ten PPCs reports that the pastor appoints the other officers. Another one in ten say either that the PPC chairperson appoints the other officers or they use some other method to select the other officers.

Most of the PPCs in our sample have a relationship with the parish finance council. The most common situation (38 percent of respondents) is for a member of the PFC to sit as a voting member of the PPC. In another 13 percent a PFC representative is a nonvoting member of the PPC. In 8 percent of the responding parishes there was a large degree of overlap among the membership of the two groups, and in 19 percent of the responding PPCs, a PFC member was not represented on the PPC.

Membership on the Parish Pastoral Council

The typical PPC has approximately 12 members, among them 1.4 clergy members, 10.8 lay members, and no members who are religious brothers or sisters. With the decline in the number of women religious and brothers serving in parish ministry, today only about 1 in 40 parishes has a religious sister or brother on the pastoral council. Table 3.3 shows that pastoral council size varies somewhat among parishes of different sizes, regions of the country, urban/rural location, as well as the type of parish leadership. On average, larger parishes, parishes in the Northeast, more urban parishes, and parishes in which the pastor is not shared with another parish tend to have 13 to 15 pastoral council members.

Selection of Members

The most common pattern for arriving at membership on the pastoral council is to elect at least some of the members from the

2. Note that only 24 responding parishes that are entrusted to a Parish Life Coordinator answered this question about who chairs the PPC meetings. This number is too small for statistical significance but may still allude to an important difference between parishes with a Pastor and those with a Parish Life Coordinator.

parish at large. Typically, the parish bulletin announces the date of the election and invites parishioners to submit their name or the name of another suitable parishioner for service on the pastoral council. These names are usually vetted by the pastor and a

Table 3.3 Size of the Parish Pastoral Council, by Selected Parish Characteristics

	Average Number of Members
Number of Households	
Less than 300	9.6
300 to 699	11.7
700 to 1,399	14.1
1,400 and over	14.6
Census Region	
Northeast	13.9
Midwest	11.1
South	12.9
West	12.7
Location	
Large City (over 100,000)	14.3
Suburb of large city	13.8
Small city or its suburb	13.9
Large town (10,000-50,000)	13.3
Small town (under 10,000)	11.2
Rural	9.8
Leadership	
Pastor of only this parish	13.5
Pastor of multiple parishes	10.5
Parish life coordinator	10.9
Entire Sample	***12.4***

nominations committee of the pastoral council and then a slate of candidates is prepared. A voting date is set by the pastoral council, often a Sunday for the convenience of registered Mass-attending parishioners, and all registered parishioners are encouraged to vote from the slate of candidates. Half of responding parishes report that they have members who are elected at large.

Some parishes have a more complicated system, whereby parishioners are invited to submit names for pastoral council membership through a discernment model. A third of responding parishes report that they have members who are discerned from a group of candidates. This is the way the discernment model operates in one diocese, according to its Pastoral Plan:

> Because the pastoral council is a visioning body ... it is recommended that members of the council be called forth from the community by a selection process that includes communal prayer and is guided by a facilitator who is skilled in the process of discernment. Each parish will determine the criteria for council membership as well as the length of service and the necessary provisions for replacement of members due to resignation, etc.

Another quarter of responding parishes report that the parish pastoral council also includes representative members that are sent by parish organizations or committees. These representative members may be selected by members within the parish organizations or committees or they may be appointed by the pastor to represent the organizations or committees.

About four in ten pastoral councils have at least one council member that is appointed by the pastor. If the pastoral council does not include representative members from parish organizations or committees, the pastor may appoint one or more members from those groups to a term. Appointed members may also be selected by the pastor from among registered parishioners at large in order to improve the balance among desired pastoral council characteristics. This is the way appointive members are described in the Pastoral Council Constitution and Bylaws of one archdiocese:

Appointive members of the Council are appointed by the Pastor. The Pastor shall name no more than three lay persons to the Council for a two year term of office. Such appointments shall endeavor to maintain a proper balance among sexes, ethnic groups, age groups, and areas of knowledge and competence desired on the Council. Appointive members shall have full voice and vote in council sessions.

Many parish pastoral councils have some members that are neither elected nor appointed but serve on the council *ex officio* by virtue of their position in the parish. Half of responding parishes include some members that serve *ex officio*. Some examples of *ex officio* members may include the pastor, priest(s) and religious sisters or brothers regularly assigned to the parish, permanent deacons, and the director of religious education, principal of the parish school, youth minister, and other staff person(s) involved in the direct pastoral care of parishioners. Typically, *ex officio* members have full voice in council discussions but do not vote.

Table 3.4 pools the responses to our survey questions about selection methods for parish pastoral council members and then displays in the first column the average proportion of all PPC members that are selected by each method. A second column reports the percentage of all PPCs that have at least one council member selected by each method. In other words, across all responding parish pastoral councils, about a third of all council members are elected at large (34 percent), a quarter are discerned from a group of candidates (24 percent), 14 percent are appointed by the pastor, and about 10 percent each are representatives of parish organizations or committees, ex officio members, or members selected some other way.

Most PPCs use some combination of these methods for selecting council members, electing some of the members, appointing others, and sending some representatives from parish organizations or committees. Only one in ten responding PPCs have all council members either elected at large or discerned from a group of candidates (not shown in the table). Small parishes (less than 300 households), parishes in the South, located in small towns and

Table 3.4 Means of Selecting Pastoral Council Members

	Average Proportion of Members Chosen This Way	Percentage of Councils with at Least One Member Chosen This Way
Elected at Large	34.2%	49%
Discerned from a Group of Candidates	24.2	32
Appointed by the Pastor	14.0	38
Representative Members Sent by Parish Organizations or Committees	10.0	25
Serving *Ex Officio* (e.g., Parish Staff)	9.5	49
Chosen Some Other Way	8.1	11

N=505 Parishes

rural areas, and parishes that share their pastor with one or more other parishes tend to have a greater than average percentage of their PPC members elected at large. By contrast, very large parishes (1,400 households and over), parishes in the West, and parishes in the suburbs around large cities tend to have a greater than average percentage of their PPC members that are discerned from a group of candidates.

Length of Term

Eight in ten responding parishes indicate that parish pastoral council members serve a term of two or more years. Another 17 percent said that they do not specify a term for pastoral council members. Only 3 percent report that the council term is for one year or less.

Meeting Procedures

As we saw in Chapter Two, important procedural issues that need to be addressed include the frequency of meetings, the extent to which council meetings are open to non-council members, and questions concerning who sets the agenda and typical agenda items.

Frequency of Meetings

In two-thirds of responding parishes the parish pastoral council meets monthly. About one in six (16 percent) indicate that the pastoral council meets bi-monthly, and 13 percent say that it meets quarterly. Very few pastoral councils meet less frequently than quarterly.

When asked about the frequency of meetings, 96 percent agree that the frequency with which the pastoral council meetings occur is sufficient for the needs of the parish. Among those who say that the frequency of meetings is not sufficient, three-quarters say that the PPC should meet more frequently and one-quarter thinks that the PPC should meet less frequently.

Open meetings

One way to encourage greater awareness of the work of the parish pastoral council among parishioners in general is by holding meetings that are open to the general public. Nearly eight in ten parishes (78 percent) say that the parish pastoral council occasionally holds open meetings. Among those that hold open meetings, half (49 percent) say the open meeting occurs monthly. About 10 percent each say that an open meeting occurs bi-monthly, quarterly, or annually. Four percent hold a semi-annual open meeting and 15 percent hold an annual meeting on some other schedule.

Meeting Agenda

Regardless who chairs the PPC meetings, more than half (52 percent) report that both the pastor and the PPC chairperson together collaborate to create the PPC agenda. Very large parishes (1,400 households or more), parishes in the West, and parishes in the suburbs or in a small city are more likely to report this collaboration on the meeting agenda. If the agenda is not created collaboratively, in 28 percent of PPCs it is the pastor who creates the agenda, and in the remaining 20 percent of PPCs the agenda is the responsibility of the PPC chairperson. The pastor is more likely to be responsible for creating the agenda if the parish is small (less than 700 households), located in the Midwest, in a rural area, and in parishes in which he is responsible for more than one parish.

The parish pastoral council members themselves most often submit items for the PPC agenda (82 percent), followed closely by the Pastor or Parish Life Coordinator. Eighty percent of responding PPCs report that the Pastor/PLC submits agenda items. Parishioners and parish staffs are also able to submit agenda items in most parish pastoral councils. Seven in ten report that parishioners can submit agenda items and 65 percent say that parish staff members can do so as well.

Typically, the PPC meeting agenda includes prayer, issues for recommendation or decision, and committee or ministry reports. Most also include issues for in-depth discussion, as can be seen in Figure 3.2.

Less commonly, the agenda may include education or formation for the PPC members, faith sharing, or social time. About a quarter to a third of PPCs report that formation, faith sharing, or

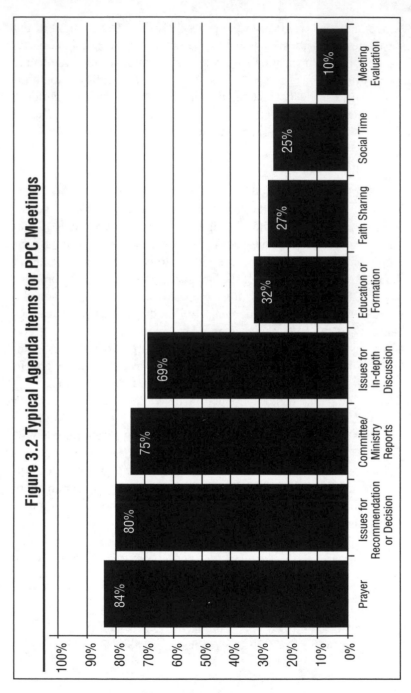

Figure 3.2 Typical Agenda Items for PPC Meetings

social time is a typical part of the agenda. Only one in ten include a meeting evaluation on the agenda.

Decision-Making Processes

Most PPCs (74 percent) say that when there are conclusions or recommendations to be made concerning major issues, the parish pastoral council uses group consensus to reach its conclusions or recommendations. Less than a quarter (23 percent) use majority vote to arrive at conclusions or recommendations of the pastoral council and very few (only 3 percent) use some sort of formal discernment model to arrive at conclusions or recommendations.

Regardless of how the pastoral council goes about making its decisions and despite the fact that 80 percent of PPCs say that issues for recommendation or decision are a typical part of their agenda, the types of decisions that PPCs make are limited in scope. For example, only 7 percent of PPCs are "very" involved in decisions about hiring parish staff, and, on average, PPCs report that they are "only a little" involved in these decisions. Likewise, a fifth of PPCs say they are "very" involved in advising parish committees, and about a quarter say they are very involved in establishing parish programs. In fact, less than half (47 percent) say that they are "very" involved in setting parish priorities, although the average PPC says it is at least somewhat involved in these decisions.

Parish Finance Councils

In Chapter Two we saw that there are three dimensions associated with parish finance councils: membership, meetings, and responsibilities. What did our survey learn about the PFCs in our sample with regards to each of these dimensions?

Membership

As noted in Chapter Two, the membership dimension of a PFC differs significantly from that of a PPC, primarily because the former requires specialized knowledge and the latter requires general knowledge. Based on that, we would expect a PFC to be a smaller, more tightly controlled group, staffed primarily by professionals. What did our survey find?

The median size of the PFCs in our sample is six members, with about half having between five and seven members. Eight percent have three or fewer members, while 10 percent of the PFCs have ten members or more.

In 63 percent of the cases, the pastor solicits parishioners to sit on the PFC. Other frequent selection methods include nomination by current PFC members (21 percent of the PFCs) and nomination by the PPC (eight percent). There were no member term limits specified among about half of the responding PFCs.

Only slightly more than half (53 percent) of the parishes in our sample have a business manager. Of these, in 28 percent of the cases the parish business manager is a voting member of the PFC; 57 percent of the time the business manager is a nonvoting member; and, somewhat curiously, in the other 15 percent of the parishes the business manager is not a member of the PFC.

Nearly two-thirds (64 percent) of the PFCs in our sample include at least one certified public accountant. Other notable professions that were represented on the PFCs in our sample include bankers (35 percent of the PFCs have at least one), brokers (15 percent), attorneys (23 percent), and other financial professionals (54 percent).

Meetings

The meetings dimension of PFCs includes the issue of meeting frequency and the question of who chairs the meeting.

Forty percent of the PFCs in our sample meet monthly. Another 15 percent meet every other month, while 34 percent meet quarterly. At the other extreme, 6 percent of the PFCs meet only twice a year, and 1 percent meet annually.

When asked if they think that the frequency of the PFC meetings is adequate, 94 percent agree. Of those who indicate that the meeting frequency is inadequate, 79 percent think that the PFC should meet more frequently, while 21 percent express the opinion that they should meet less often.

Responses to the question of who chairs the PFC meeting are fairly evenly split among the pastor (35 percent), a chair elected by the PFC members (34 percent), and an appointed chairperson (26 percent). Presumably, in this case the chairperson would have been appointed by the pastor.

Responsibilities

As mentioned in Chapter Two, PFCs have three responsibilities: maintaining and enforcing internal financial controls; evaluating and reviewing parish financial statements; and, where appropriate, involvement in parish decisions that have financial implications. Chapter Four is concerned with parish internal financial controls, so only the latter two of these responsibilities are discussed here.

Evaluating and Reviewing Parish Financial Statements

From Table 3.5 we can see that a little less than three-fourths of the PFCs in our sample review important parish financial statements, such as cash receipts and disbursements, cash on hand, the balance sheet, and actual to budgeted comparisons, at least quarterly, with more than 40 percent reviewing them monthly. Other financial statements, including the unpaid bills and the amount of debt outstanding, are reviewed slightly less frequently. What is of concern, however, is the fairly substantial number of PFCs that *never* review such fundamental financial statements like the amount of unpaid bills (39 percent of PFCs), periodic cash receipts and disbursements (15 percent), the amount of debt outstanding and the amount of cash on hand (each 11 percent), and even the balance sheet (6 percent). One certainly has to wonder how a PFC

Table 3.5 Frequency of Financial Statements Review

	Monthly	Quarterly	Yearly	Never
Periodic cash receipts and disbursements	42%	30%	7%	15%
Year-to-date cash receipts and disbursements	42	33	9	10
Amount of unpaid bills at end of period	28	21	7	39
Amount of cash on hand	42	32	9	11
Balance sheet	42	34	12	6
Comparison of actual to budget	42	37	9	7
Comparison of current to prior year	30	29	25	7
Amount of debt outstanding	38	32	12	11

Table 3.6 Involvement in Parish Financial Decisions

	Consults	Determines	Approves	Not Involved
Hiring/Firing senior parish staff	36%	0%	6%	57%
Contract with outside vendors	44	5	17	34
Parish operating budget	28	19	51	3
Parish financial policy	38	19	39	5
Long-range parish financial/physical needs	45	22	29	4

can perform its function under Canon Law if it *never* evaluates and reviews these critical financial statements.

Other Parish Financial Decisions

Depending on the situation (including whether or not the parish has a business manager), the PFC might be involved in other parish decisions that have financial ramifications. This involvement might range from merely consulting on a decision to having final approval. In many cases, PFCs might not be involved at all.

Table 3.6 shows the responses to the question of the level of involvement in five types of parish decisions that have financial implications.

Generally speaking, PFCs are involved in one form or another in a broad range of parish financial decisions. As would be expected, they are most involved in establishing the parish budget, where more than half have final approval and only 3 percent are not involved at all. They also tend to be heavily involved in planning, both in setting a parish financial policy and in planning for the long-term financial and physical needs of the parish. Not surprisingly, PFCs are least involved in the hiring or firing of senior staff, a responsibility that typically falls on the pastor.

Education and Formation of PFC Members

As with PPC members discussed above, we inquired about the types of education and formation activities that are available to PFC members. Table 3.7 shows both the sources and the types of education and formation received by PFC members.

After a quick glance at Table 3.7, one is immediately struck by the dearth of education and formation available to members of this critically important parish ministry. One can argue that PFC members tend to be highly trained professionals who are applying their training to the parish, and thus are in less need of education than members of other parish ministries. However, clearly the financial needs of a nonprofit (not to mention one that is faith-based) differ from those in the proprietary sector, where most PFC members

Table 3.7 Parish Finance Council Education/Formation Activities

	Percentage of PFCs Responding
Source of Education/Formation	
Diocesan consulting support	26%
Parish-based education/formation programs	26
Orientation program offered by diocese	21
Diocesan-sponsored formation programs (retreats, etc.)	9
Type of Education/Formation	
Financial management	48%
Issues of physical property (real estate, insurance, etc.)	29
Canon Law	23
Theology of the parish	20
Investments	20
Human resource management	16
Group process	14
Personal spirituality	11

received their experience. Not all PFC members are financial professionals. Few would have any background in Canon Law, which is the underpinning of the council's very existence. And if serving as a member of a PFC is to be viewed as a ministry, rather than merely a volunteer activity, at least some emphasis needs to be placed on topics like the theology of the parish and each member's personal spirituality.

Of special concern is the failure on the part of most dioceses to offer consulting support to assist PFCs in dealing with some of the intricacies of parish finances. Other studies have shown that in many cases, neither the pastor nor the parish business manager (where one exists) is comfortable in their understanding of many of these issues (Zech and Miller, 2007).

Summary

Despite the fact that parish pastoral councils receive little mention in Canon Law, they have achieved widespread acceptance in parishes in the United States since Vatican II, and today most parishes have some sort of pastoral council. Similarly, although little is written about them and they are structured according to norms established by each diocesan bishop, these pastoral councils are surprisingly similar in size, structure, and function. In contrast, parish finance councils *do* have their basis in Canon Law, and we also found many similarities across PFCs in the way their members are selected, how they conduct their meetings, and the responsibilities that they assume.

This chapter described typical characteristics of the parishes included in this study as well as the typical characteristics of their parish pastoral council and parish finance council. We examined these characteristics according to the five dimensions of parish pastoral councils and the three dimensions of parish finance councils as presented in Chapter Two. The next chapter will examine more thoroughly how well the parish finance council operates to ensure that proper internal financial controls are in place in the parish.

Chapter Four

Parish Internal Financial Controls

An important function of the Parish Finance Council is to ensure that proper internal financial controls are in place in the parish. Newspaper headlines in recent years have revealed an alarming number of fraud and embezzlement cases involving Catholic clergy and church workers. Most of these have occurred at the parish level. Among the more sensational cases that have emerged in the last few years are:

- The parish administrator of the Basilica of the National Shrine of the Assumption of the Blessed Virgin Mary in the Archdiocese of Baltimore was accused of embezzling $443,000 over a three-year period.
- A parish employee in the Diocese of San Antonio, Texas, pleaded guilty to stealing over $472,000 in parish funds.
- A parish business manager in the Diocese of Little Rock, Arkansas, was charged with stealing over $499,000.
- A priest of the Diocese of Worcester, Massachusetts, was charged with stealing more than $250,000 from his parish.
- A priest of the Diocese of Brooklyn, New York, was accused of stealing nearly $2 million from his parish between 1982 and 1999.
- A bookkeeper at a parish in Florida was accused of embezzling $675,000 from her parish.
- A priest who served as the principal of a Philadelphia Catholic high school pleaded guilty to embezzling $900,000 from the school and from his religious order.
- A priest in Connecticut was accused of embezzling $1.2 million from his parish.

- A priest from New Jersey was accused of embezzling $2 million from his parish.
- Two priests from the same parish in Florida were accused of embezzling over $10 million from their parish.

In fact, a survey conducted by Robert West and Charles Zech (2008) of diocesan chief financial officers revealed that 85 percent of U.S. Catholic dioceses that responded to the survey reported that they had one or more embezzlements in the recent past. In 23 percent of the cases, the embezzlement was discovered by a member of the parish finance council.

Perhaps we shouldn't be too shocked when we learn of church workers and clergy caving in to the temptation inherent in the care of church resources. This has been a problem from the very beginning. In John 12:6, referring to Judas Iscariot, the Gospel writer states, "...he was a thief. He carried the money bag and would help himself from it."

Whenever one learns of a large embezzlement at the parish level, one of the first questions that should be asked is, "Where was the parish finance council?" In order to emphasize the parish finance council's responsibility with regards to parish internal financial controls, the USCCB, at its November 2007 meeting, approved a statement by its Ad Hoc Committee on Diocesan Audits. In addition to calling for annual internal audits of each parish, the statement (p. 3) called for an annual parish financial report, signed by the pastor and all parish finance council members, to be submitted to the diocese. This financial report should include the parish's financial statements for the fiscal year, its prospective budget, and most important in terms of the topic of this chapter, an attestation that the signers affirm that the financial statements, to the best of their knowledge, accurately reflect the financial condition of the parish, that the parish finance council has reviewed and approved the financial statements and the budget, and that the signers have not received any credible report that has not been reported to the diocesan bishop or his delegate of fraud, abuse, or misappropriation. This document clearly places parish internal financial controls within the arena of responsibility of the parish finance council.

Typically, embezzlements occur when trusted employees, such as church workers or clergy, have access to both assets **and** financial records. Most parishes have relatively few staff members. This presents two problems: they have difficulty separating duties, and employees often have little supervision by a qualified financial manager. A basic principle of internal accounting controls is to keep the financial recordkeeping duties separate from those individuals that have access to assets, especially cash.

The threat of embezzlements caused by the difficulty parishes have in separating duties is intensified by two other factors. One is the fact that pastors, and in some cases parish business managers, have little or no training in accounting or business practices. No one became a priest because he wanted to run a small business (a parish). Likewise, many parish business managers (where they exist) are unfamiliar with the special needs of a nonprofit organization that is run on primarily a cash basis.

An additional concern is that, as a faith-based organization, parishes can be too trusting. No one would ordinarily expect a priest or lay church worker to engage in embezzlement. Internal financial controls might be viewed as unnecessary in parishes. In fact, priests and parish workers might consider it insulting even to imply that internal financial controls are important. Therefore, controls that are routinely put into place in the business sector are often resisted in parishes.

Nevertheless, the necessity of putting into place internal financial controls to thwart embezzlement is an issue that the U.S. Catholic bishops have taken very seriously. In the following sections of this chapter we examine the USCCB's recommended policies and procedures regarding internal financial controls and examine our survey data to learn the extent to which parishes in our sample are adhering to those policies and procedures.

United States Conference of Catholic Bishops' Policies on Internal Financial Controls

As mentioned above, the U.S. Catholic bishops take the threat of embezzlements very seriously. In 1992 the U.S. Catholic Conference (as they were then known) directed its Accounting Practices Committee to study and propose diocesan internal financial control policies. In 1995, the USCC approved a document entitled "Diocesan Internal Controls: A Framework." In the Foreword to this document, Canon 1284 of the *Code of Canon Law* is cited. This Canon requires Church administrators to carry out their responsibilities with the prudence of a "good householder." Individual bishops can delegate the authority, but not the responsibility, to implement sound internal financial controls.

The Foreword makes it clear that the document addresses diocesan level issues and does not specifically deal with parish issues. However, it also notes that parishes would find the guidance contained in the document to be useful. It is important to note that this document, like all USCCB recommendations, contains just that, recommendations. Individual dioceses are free to implement all, some, or none of them.

Later in the document (p.6) it is recognized that diocesan finance councils should have a significant role in the internal financial control functions of a diocese. By extension, since parish finance councils are also mandated by Canon Law, they, too, bear responsibility for internal financial controls at the parish level. The document then proceeds (pp. 8-9) to lay out the basic elements of a sound internal financial controls system. They are adapted here to apply to parishes.

1. Honest and capable employees. Nearly all embezzlements have been committed by individuals who have been granted a great deal of trust. If a person is dishonest, even the best control system might not perform properly. Among the recommendations listed are:

- Require annual vacations to ensure that any fraud requiring a staff member's constant attention could be discovered.
- Establish and educate staff on conflict-of-interest policies.
- Watch for signs that a staff member is spending more than his/her salary would typically permit. Many

times embezzlement occurs to feed an addiction (e.g. gambling, alcohol) or when individuals find themselves in serious debt.

2. Delegation and separation of duties. The system should provide for clear segregation of duties between the custody of and the accountability for assets. For example, the custody of assets should be separated from the record keeping of those assets. Authorizing transactions should be separate from recording the transaction. If the parish staff is too small to make the segregation of duties practical, a member of the parish finance council should oversee the activities.

3. Procedures for processing of transactions. A basic element of internal financial controls is proper authorization. The day-to-day operating authority that has been delegated to the appropriate individuals should include specific guidelines that need to be followed.

4. Suitable documents and accounting records. Records should be maintained to provide an accounting trail. The supporting documentation should be simple and easy to use and numbered to help keep physical control over the documents.

5. Physical control over assets and accounting records. Accounting records should be protected by physical barriers, such as locked drawers. Access to computer equipment and software should be controlled and backup files stored off-site. Physical assets, such as furniture or equipment, should be numbered and inventoried.

6. Independent verification of performance. Procedures need to be in place to reconcile actual transactions with those transactions that have been recorded.

The document notes (p. 7) that external auditors can be helpful in reporting material differences in internal control systems and their implementation. However, external auditors should not be relied on to identify all weaknesses, unless the auditors have been specifically engaged to review the system.

Among the specific recommendations listed in the document (pp. 9-12), again, adapted here to apply to parishes, are:

1. Parishes should be required to adhere to a prescribed budget process, resulting in an annual budget.

2. Periodically parishes should report operating results versus budgeted amounts.

3. Monthly comparative financial statements should be prepared so that appropriate action could be taken if the actual results vary materially from those budgeted.

4. Establish policy and procedures manuals to ensure that similar transactions are handled in similar manners.

5. The number of bank accounts should be strictly limited to allow greater control and less opportunity for error or wrongdoing.

6. Authorized check signers should be very limited.

7. Checks in large amounts should require the signature of two responsible individuals.

8. Bank statements should be reconciled by someone other than the check signers.

9. Checks should be drawn according to procedures prescribing adequate supporting documentation.

Survey Findings

What did our survey find concerning the implementation of the Accounting Practices Committee's recommendations?

Parishes should be required to adhere to a prescribed budget process, resulting in an annual budget.

As Table 4.1 indicates, over 90 percent of the parishes in our sample prepare an annual operating budget. Among those that prepare

Table 4.1 Parish Budget Process

	Percentage of PFCs Responding
A parish operating budget projecting income and expenditures is prepared annually	91%
Of those parishes preparing a budget, role of the Parish Finance Council in the budgetary process:	
Approves	53%
Consults	26
Determines	19
Not involved	2
Of those parishes preparing a budget, parish involvement in budget process:	
Ask parish ministries about their financial needs	76%
Presentation of draft budget for PPC feedback	49
Explanation of draft budget in bulletin	14
Explanation of draft budget presented at Mass	10
Open parish hearings to establish budget priorities	9
Presentation of draft budget for parishioner feedback	4
Explanation of draft budget in parish newsletter	4
Explanation of draft budget mailed to parishioners	4

a budget, the parish finance council was involved at some level in all but 2 percent of the parishes. That's the good news. On the other hand, the vast majority of the parishes in our sample failed to make any attempt to extend the budget process parishwide or to achieve parishioner involvement. Broader participation would contribute to greater oversight and a decreased opportunity for embezzlement.

Periodically, parishes should report operating results compared to budgeted amounts. Also, monthly comparative financial statements should be prepared so that appropriate action could be taken if the actual results vary materially from those budgeted.

In Table 4.2 we find that fewer than half of the parish finance councils report that they review actual versus budgeted amounts monthly, but over 80 percent of them do so at least quarterly. Even fewer (32 percent monthly, 62 percent at least quarterly) regularly compare this year's budgeted amounts to those of a prior year. In addition to reporting operating results on a timely basis, the Accounting Practices Committee recommended monthly reporting of other financial statements. As Table 4.2 shows, while upwards of three quarters of the PFCs in our survey reviewed their balance sheets at least quarterly, fewer than half met the monthly standard set by the Accounting Practices Committee.

A small minority report their financial statements to the parish at large on a timely basis, and in many cases, these reports are not made available to the entire parish at all.

Establish policy and procedures manuals to ensure that similar transactions are handled in similar manners.

A majority of parishes follow a manual that spells out the responsibilities of the PFC, and a large number follows an accounting procedures manual. In both cases, about two-thirds of the parishes use materials provided by the diocese.

But in Table 4.3, we find a disturbing pattern. One-sixth of the parishes in our sample do not adhere to a policies manual for

Table 4.2 Parishes with an Operating Budget: Budget Comparisons

	Monthly	Quarterly	Yearly	Other	Never
Parish Finance Council reviews:					
Comparison of actual to budgeted amounts	44%	39%	9%	5%	3%
Comparison of current year amounts to prior year	32	30	25	8	5
Balance sheet	44	36	10	6	4
Parish Finance Council reports to parishioners:					
Comparison of actual to budgeted amounts	8%	11%	46%	8%	27%
Comparison of current year amounts to prior year	5	6	48	9	32
Balance sheet	6	9	53	6	27

Table 4.3 Parish Employs Policies/Procedures Manuals

	Percentage of PFCs Responding
PFC follows a policies/guidelines manual spelling out its responsibilities:	
Yes, use manual developed by diocese	66%
Yes, use manual that we developed ourselves	14
Yes, use manual developed by another agency	3
No	17
Parish follows an accounting procedures manual:	
Yes, use manual developed by diocese	69%
Yes, use manual that we developed ourselves	7
Yes, use manual developed by another agency	7
No	17

its PFC, and a similar number fail to follow any accounting procedures manual. At least in the latter case, this is a serious violation of good internal financial controls practices, and opens these parishes to the threat of fraud and embezzlement by its staff.

The number of bank accounts should be strictly limited to allow greater control and less opportunity for error or wrongdoing.

We did not ask our sample how many checking accounts the parish held, only whether they had one, or more than one, other than checking accounts held for the parochial school, which should be separate. More than half of the parishes indicated that they only hold a single checking account (Table 4.4). But more than 40 percent had more than one checking account, presumably held by in-

Table 4.4 Parish Checking Accounts

	Percentage of PFCs Responding
Parish has a single checking account	55%
Parish has multiple checking accounts	43
Other	2

dividual parish organizations. While there could be good reasons for a parish to hold more than one checking account, this practice needs to be closely monitored. For example, papers filed in connection with the 2007 bankruptcy case of the Diocese of San Diego revealed that parishes in that diocese held an average of eight checking accounts. This can be a very dangerous practice and could lead to abuse of the system.

Authorized check signers should be very limited, and checks in large amounts should require the signature of two responsible individuals.

In Table 4.5 we see who in the parish is authorized to sign checks. To no one's surprise, the person most frequently authorized to sign checks is the pastor. This is as it should be, since the pastor is ultimately responsible for the parish's finances. But this does beg the question as to why this figure is not 100 percent. In fact, 7 percent of the pastors in our sample do not have the authority to write checks on behalf of the parish. One possible explanation for this discrepancy is that the parish has a nontraditional pastoral leadership arrangement, either belonging to a cluster or served by a parish life coordinator. Upon closer examination, this is the case for over half of the parishes in our sample for whom the pastor was not authorized to sign checks (a third were clustered and 20 percent were served by a PLC). But the other 47 percent of the parishes in our sample for whom the pastor did not have check-signing authority were served by a resident priest-pastor.

Table 4.5 Authorized Check Signers

	Percentage of PFCs Responding
Pastor	93%
Bookkeeper	11
Business Manager	12
PFC Member	8
Other Staff	13
Parishioner nonstaff	4
Total authorized check signers in parish:	
One	65%
Two	29
Three	5
Four	<1
Five	<1
Average number of authorized check signers = 1.41	

The second most likely person in a parish to have check-signing authority was not the parish bookkeeper or the parish business manager, but rather some other parish staff member. Another curious finding was that in 4 percent of the parishes, a parishioner who is not a staff member had the authority to sign checks.

A related issue concerns the number of signers required for large disbursements. While it is bad practice for internal financial control to have too many individuals with the authority to sign checks, it is also of concern when only one person's signature is needed on large checks. Again referring to Table 4.5, the average number of authorized check signers in our sample was 1.4. In two-thirds of the parishes in our sample, only one person was authorized to sign checks, no matter how large the amount. Clearly, this should be of concern.

Table 4.6 Parish Bank Reconciliations

	Percentage of PFCs Responding
Number of individuals who perform bank reconciliations:	
One	80%
Two	17
Three	3
Four	<1
Percent of parishes in which lone individual both performs reconciliation and also	
Signs checks	
Pastor	3%
Bookkeeper	4
Business Manager	2
Deposits collections	
Pastor	1%
Bookkeeper	11
Business Manager	5
Makes other deposits	
Pastor	2%
Bookkeeper	21
Business Manager	9
Approves routine disbursements	
Pastor	3%
Bookkeeper	25
Business Manager	12
Approves nonbudgeted disbursements	
Pastor	3%
Bookkeeper	1
Business Manager	2

Bank statements should be reconciled by someone other than the check signers.

We asked our sample about various individuals within the parish who performed bank reconciliations. As the top of Table 4.6 indicates, 80 percent of the parishes assigned that task to one individual. This, by itself, is not necessarily bad, since it allows for consistency and continuity. But it is a concern when it results in a loss of separation of duties and independent verification of performance.

Our survey also asked about a number of routine parish financial transactions and information concerning who was responsible for these transactions. In the lower portion of Table 4.6, we identify the percentage of parishes in which **the same individual** was the sole person in the parish responsible for reconciling the bank statements and for five different routine parish financial transactions. Any time these appear in combination, there is a clear violation of separation of duties and independent verification of performance.

In Table 4.6, we find that in about 9 percent of the parishes in our sample, the same person had sole responsibility for both writing checks and reconciling bank statements. In about one-sixth of the parishes, the same person was solely responsible for depositing the Sunday collection and for reconciling bank statements, and in nearly a third of the parishes only one person deposited non-collection revenues and reconciled the bank statements. Some 40 percent of the parishes gave one person the sole authority to both approve routine disbursements and reconcile bank statements, and 6 percent gave the responsibility to a single individual for both approving nonbudgeted expenditures and reconciling bank statements.

The lack of separation of duties and verification of performance represented by these findings is a matter for concern. Parishes that fail to separate the task of bank reconciliation from these routine financial transactions make it easy for someone to succumb to the temptation to embezzle funds.

A related issue concerns the status of the individuals who count the Sunday collection. Consistent with the spirit of sepa-

Table 4.7 Parish Collection Counters

	Percentage of PFCs Responding
Parish has a single individual counting the collection:	
Pastor	1%
Other parish staff member	4
Parish has a regular counting crew to count the collection:	
Regular counting crew with no staff members (mean = 1.06)	48%
Regular counting crew with no volunteers (mean = 3.99)	10
Parish has rotating counting crews to count the collection:	
Rotating counting crews with no staff members (mean = .59)	69%
Rotating counting crews with no volunteers (mean = 3.37)	6

ration of duties, no one person should count the collection on a regular basis. Ideally, the parish should rely on rotating crews of counters, staffed by both parish staff and volunteers.

Table 4.7 reveals that in about 5 percent of the parishes in our sample, only one individual counts the Sunday collection. About 40 percent of the parishes employ a regular crew of counters with an average of about 5 members. But nearly half of these fail to include any staff members among the counters. Both of these approaches are fraught with danger.

The good news is that more than half the parishes in our sample utilize a system of rotating collection counting teams with an average of about four members per crew. More than two-thirds of the rotating crew parishes do not have any staff members involved in collection counting.

Checks should be drawn according to procedures prescribing adequate supporting documentation.

We asked our sample if check signers are provided documentation to support each check before they signed. Of those responding with either a yes or a no, a healthy 91 percent indicate that they are.

Parish Audits

As noted above, at its November, 2007 meeting, the USCCB approved a resolution submitted by its Ad Hoc Committee on Diocesan Audits calling for annual internal audits for all parishes. This is only a recommendation, and each diocesan ordinary is free to follow it to the degree that he chooses. On the other hand, a number of observers have called for annual **external** audits of parishes. An internal audit would typically be performed by a diocesan examiner, while an external audit would be conducted by an individual (or team) from an independent accounting firm.

The primary purpose of an audit is not to discover fraud. At the same time, the belief is that if parish staff knew that the parish books were subject to an outside control mechanism like audits, they would be more reluctant to engage in fraud. In any event, auditors are capable of recognizing reporting errors and deficiencies in internal financial controls. These could be highlighted in Management Letter Comments that accompany the audit and that alert the diocese of the need for corrective action in the parish. Management letter comments are written even if a "violation" did not occur but the auditors believe the controls are such that the parish risks a violation if the controls are not strengthened. In order to be most effective, audits should occur regularly and randomly.

The Ad Hoc Committee recognized (pp. 3-4) that annual audits of parishes, even internal audits, can be expensive and could place a financial burden on many dioceses. To help ease the burden, the Committee recognized three models for annual audits:

1. The best practice would be for the diocese to hire internal staff to audit parishes and report directly to an independent accounting/auditing committee and the diocesan ordinary.

2. An alternative would be to audit every parish every two or three years, or when the pastor changes, using part-time internal staff or by outsourcing the audit function to independent CPAs. Under this model, the auditor would report to the pastor, the parish finance council, and the bishop.

3. At a minimum, the Committee recommended using retired or volunteer CPAs to conduct reviews of parish finances. As a last resort, the parish finance council would perform internal financial reviews.

Models two and three, while perhaps financially necessary in some dioceses, fall well short of the standards needed to ensure confidence in parish financial dealings.

We asked our sample about the frequency with which parish audits (either internal or external) occur. The results can be found in Table 4.8. About a quarter of our respondents claim to be audited annually. At the other end of the spectrum, about 15 percent of the parishes are never audited. The most frequent response to the audit question was "Other."

Table 4.8 Frequency of Diocesan Financial Audits	Percentage of PFCs Responding
Annually	26%
Every two years	7
Every three years	20
Other	32
Never	15

This generally means that parishes are audited on an irregular basis, typically when a pastor or bookkeeper leaves the parish. In fact, some of the largest embezzlement cases in recent years have occurred in parishes where the pastor had been in place for many years without the parish having been subjected to an audit. It was only when the pastor was reassigned or died, and the parish was subject to an audit, that the fraud was discovered.

As disconcerting as it is to learn that three-fourths of all parishes in our sample are audited less than annually (and 15 percent are **never** audited), these figures probably still exaggerate the number of parish audits that are taking place nationwide. In their survey of diocesan chief financial officers, West and Zech (2008) found that only 3 percent of responding dioceses audit their parishes annually. Twenty-one percent indicated that they never audit their parishes, and 14 percent audit their parishes only in the event of a change in pastor or other key staff member, such as the parish bookkeeper or parish business manager.

Whether the results of this survey are accurate, the results of the West/Zech survey are accurate, or the truth lies somewhere in between, we should still be concerned. Clearly, diocesan ordinaries do not seem to be taking the recommendation by the USCCB Ad Hoc Committee on Diocesan Audits to audit every parish annually very seriously.

Summary

Because of the nature of parish life, parishes are especially susceptible to fraud. They are primarily cash-based, and parishioners tend to place an inordinate amount of trust in their clergy and parish workers. In addition, many parishes are short of staff, which makes it difficult for them to separate financial duties and provide the appropriate amount of managerial oversight.

To their credit, the USCCB, through various committees, has recognized the threat and has developed a set of common-sense recommendations to deal with the problem. However, diocesan ordinaries can choose to implement all, none, or only some of these recommendations.

The data reported in this chapter show that many parishes routinely violate some of these recommendations. It is incumbent upon all diocesan ordinaries to recognize the harm to the reputation of the Church when even minor transgressions are discovered, and to implement the recommendations approved by their national body. But implementation may not be enough. Each diocese must regularly monitor their parishes to ensure that basic internal financial controls are in place and are being utilized effectively.

In the next chapter, we examine the relationships between parish pastoral councils and parish finance councils. We also explore the communication that takes place between each of these consultative bodies and the parish as a whole.

Chapter Five

Relationships and Communication

Canon 212 §l. The Christian faithful, conscious of their own responsibility, are bound by Christian obedience to follow what the sacred pastors, as representatives of Christ, declare as teachers of the faith or establish as leaders of the Church. §2. The Christian faithful are free to make known their needs, especially spiritual ones, and their desires to the pastors of the Church. §3. In accord with the knowledge, competence and preeminence which they possess, they have the right and even at times a duty to manifest to the sacred pastors their opinion on matters which pertain to the good of the Church, and they have a right to make their opinion known to the other Christian faithful, with due regard for the integrity of faith and morals and reverence toward their pastors, and with consideration for the common good and the dignity of persons.

This Canon lays out the mutual interdependence that exists between the pastor and the Christian faithful. Parishioners are obliged to follow the teaching and counsel of the pastor in his declarations as teacher of the faith and leader of the Church. Similarly, they are to make known to the pastor their spiritual needs and desires. Finally, they have the right and obligation to share their opinions with the pastor and with other parishioners about things that "pertain to the good of the Church." Although not specifically referring to the work of a parish pastoral council, the third sentence, in particular, describes the importance of communication within the community of the faithful that is the parish. This chapter examines some of the relationships among the various consultative bodies of the parish and the pastor as well as the ways that those bodies communicate with parishioners.

Relationship between Parish Pastoral Councils and Parish Finance Councils

Let us examine first how communication works between the two primary consultative bodies of the parish — the parish pastoral council and the parish finance council. Nearly all of the parishes that responded to this study (about 95 percent) have both a parish pastoral council and a parish finance council. These two bodies are independent of one another, in most cases, and their responsibilities are quite different, but they do sometimes have some overlap in membership. In addition to the pastor, who is almost always a member of both councils, four in ten parish pastoral councils (39 percent) report that one or more members of the parish finance council sit on the parish pastoral council as voting members. Another seventh (14 percent) reports that one or more finance council members sit on the pastoral council as *ex officio*, nonvoting members.

Representation of the parish pastoral council on the parish finance council is somewhat less common. About a third (32 percent) of parish finance councils report that one or more members of the parish pastoral council sit on the finance council as voting members and another tenth (11 percent) have them as *ex officio*, nonvoting members. About a fifth of each of the bodies report that there is no cross-representation — no member of the pastoral council (except the pastor) sits on the finance council and no member of the finance council sits on the pastoral council.

Rarely, the two consultative bodies overlap in a significant way or the parish finance council is subsumed as a subcommittee of the pastoral council. For example, about a seventh of parish pastoral councils (14 percent) report that the parish finance council is a subcommittee of the pastoral council, but this situation is more common among clustered parishes (17 percent of clustered parishes) than among parishes that are not clustered (just 5 percent

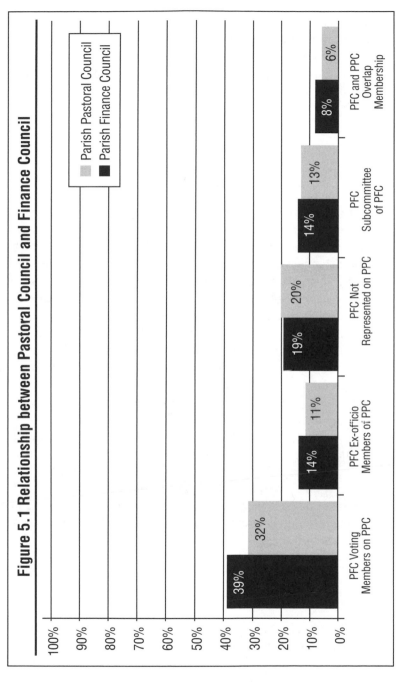

Figure 5.1 Relationship between Pastoral Council and Finance Council

Parish Pastoral Council
Parish Finance Council

100%
90%
80%
70%
60%
50%
40%
30%
20%
10%
0%

PFC Voting Members on PPC — 39%, 32%

PFC Ex-officio Members of PPC — 14%, 11%

PFC Not Represented on PPC — 19%, 20%

PFC Subcommittee of PFC — 14%, 13%

PFC and PPC Overlap Membership — 8%, 6%

report this arrangement). A more troubling finding is the fact that 8 percent of responding parishes report that the two councils are essentially the same. This situation may be problematic, in that it subordinates one council to another. There is nothing in the recommendations from Church documents that suggests this to be a good idea.

The Parish Pastoral Council and Communication within the Parish Community

We already described in Chapter Three how communication works within the pastoral council — in most cases, the pastor or parish life coordinator is a member of the pastoral council and that person typically submits agenda items for the PPC to consider. Half the time, the pastoral council also includes representation by one or more *ex officio* members from the parish staff. About a third of responding councils report one or more representatives from parish organizations or committees on the council. Parish staff, pastoral council members, and even parishioners typically (in at least two-thirds of responding parishes) are allowed to submit agenda items for the pastoral council to consider.

Usually, the pastor or parish life coordinator meets with the pastoral council chairperson to create the agenda for the pastoral council meeting and then the pastoral council chairperson chairs the council meeting. In more than 10 percent of parish pastoral councils who responded to the survey, though, both the pastor and the council chairperson conduct the meetings together. The less collaborative model, in which the pastor creates the agenda and chairs the meeting, is less common. However, when the pastor is the one who sets the agenda, 40 percent of the time he will also chair the meeting.

Communicating with the Parish

Canon 212§2 emphasizes that parishioners are to make known to the pastor their needs, especially their spiritual needs, and their

Table 5.1 Communication about the Parish Pastoral Council to the Parish

	Percentage of PPCs Responding
PPC holds open meetings (ever)	78%
PPC meetings are announced in the parish bulletin	75
PPC member contact information is published in the bulletin	66
PPC meetings are announced at Sunday Mass	38
PPC meetings are announced in a parish newsletter	11
PPC minutes are:	
Available to parishioners upon request	50%
Posted on the parish grounds	19
Posted on the parish website	12
Reported in a parish newsletter	5
Not shared with parishioners	12

desires. The parish pastoral council, insofar as it is open to parishioners, serves as an avenue for some of that communication. The responsibility for good communication with parishioners, however, is incumbent on the pastoral council. Parishioners may submit agenda items to the parish pastoral council, but are not likely to do so unless they know when the council meetings are held, who the council members are, what the process for submitting an agenda item is, and most importantly, what the parish pastoral council does.

Most parish pastoral councils use some sort of communication to announce their existence to the parish (see Table 5.1), but the practice is by no means universal. About three in four place an announcement about their upcoming meetings in the parish bulletin. Another two in three publish contact information for parish pastoral council members in the bulletin, so that interested parishioners can know how to contact their council representatives. Less commonly, about four in ten report that the council meetings are announced at Sunday Mass. Only about one in ten announce the parish pastoral council meetings in a parish newsletter.

After the pastoral council meetings, few pastoral councils do much at all to communicate with parishioners about what took place at the meeting. Half of responding pastoral councils make the minutes of the council meeting available to parishioners upon request. About a fifth post the minutes somewhere on the parish grounds and just over a tenth post the minutes on the parish website. Just as many (12 percent), though, report that the minutes are not shared with parishioners at all.

Open meetings are another way for the parish pastoral council to communicate with the parish and to familiarize parishioners with the process of consultative decision-making. This practice is also less common than one might anticipate, particularly given the obligation implied in Canon 212 to maintain open communication "on matters which pertain to the good of the Church." A little more than three in four responding councils report that they ever

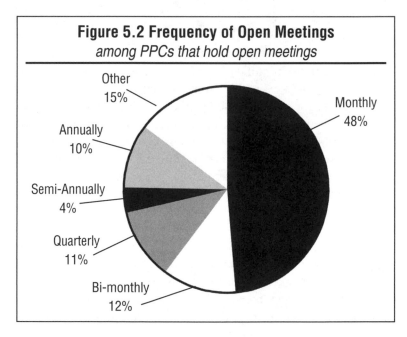

Figure 5.2 Frequency of Open Meetings
among PPCs that hold open meetings

Other 15%
Monthly 48%
Annually 10%
Semi-Annually 4%
Quarterly 11%
Bi-monthly 12%

Table 5.2 Relationship between Parish Pastoral Council and Parish Commissions, Committees, or Organizations

	Percentage of PPCs Responding
PPC receives reports from commissions, committees, or organizations	62%
PPC presents vision, goals, and priorities to guide the work and planning of those groups	40
Parish commissions, committees, or organizations submit goals and objectives to the PPC for approval	22

hold open meetings, and among those who do hold open meetings, just about half do so monthly. (See Figure 5.2.)

Communicating with the Commissions, Committees, or Organizations of the Parish

During the parish pastoral council meeting, three in four pastoral councils say they typically receive committee or ministry reports from representatives of the parish. When asked specifically about the relationship between the PPC and the various parish commissions, committees, or organizations, responding parish councils reported several ways that the activity of the parish is communicated to the pastoral council. Table 5.2 describes the percentage of responding pastoral councils that report each type of communication.

As can be seen in Table 5.2, the communication from the committees and organizations of the parish to the pastoral council about their various activities appears to be fairly regular. More than six in ten councils report that they receive reports from the various groups of the parish. At the same time, it is less clear from the data that the coordination of the mission of the parish is being communicated through these channels. Four in ten responding councils say that the parish pastoral council presents the vision, goals, and priorities to guide the work and planning of parish commissions, committees, or organizations. Even fewer, only about one in five responding councils say that these groups present their goals and objectives to the parish pastoral council for approval. This would suggest, then, that in most parishes the various parish commissions, committees, or organizations operate largely independent of the parish pastoral council, relying largely on one-way reports of action taken to simply keep the pastoral council informed.

Communicating the Vision and Mission of the Parish

Just how important is it that the parish pastoral council be involved in communicating the vision and mission of the parish? Whether the pastoral council sees itself as primarily a planning council or primarily a council of ministries, communicating the vision and mission of the parish is a vital function of the council. The survey asked councils to describe how important to the parish were 12 different functions of the parish pastoral council. A follow-up series of questions then asked them to estimate how involved the council is in each of those 12 functions.

Factor analysis of each set of questions revealed three underlying clusters of response. In other words, for both the importance of various functions and the involvement of the pastoral council in these various functions, three basic functions emerged from the statistical analysis: a **planning** function, a **coordinating** function, and a **communicating** function.

Setting the vision for the parish is included in the **planning** function of the council, along with recommending action to the pastor, planning for pastoral needs, studying issues in-depth, and developing parish policy. (See Table 5.3.) More than half of the responding councils reported that all but one of these planning functions was "very" important. Four in ten said that studying issues in-depth was a "very" important function of the council.

The most important planning function of the pastoral council — recommending action to the pastor — is seen as "very" important by two in three responding pastoral councils. More than nine in ten regard this function as at least "somewhat" important,

Table 5.3 Parish Pastoral Council Planning Functions

	Percent Important		Percent Involved		
	Somewhat	Very	Somewhat	Very	Difference
Recommending Action to the Pastor	28%	65%c	33%	58%	-7
Setting Parish Vision	26	63	34	51	-12
Planning for Pastoral Needs	30	56	39	43	-13
Developing Parish Policy	30	54	40	41	-13
Studying Issues In-Depth	42	40	40	35	-5

Table 5.4 Parish Pastoral Council Communicating Functions

	Percent Important		Percent Involved		
	Somewhat	Very	Somewhat	Very	Difference
Serving as Parish Sounding Board for Parishioners	30%	58%	32%	50%	-8
Serving as Parish Sounding Board for Pastor/Staff	28	57	33	48	-9
Serving as Parish Sounding Board for Parish Groups	35	50	37	42	-8

and the same proportion report that the pastoral council is at least "somewhat" involved in this function. However, while two-thirds see this as a "very" important function of the council, fewer than six in ten say that the council is "very" involved in recommending action to the pastor — a difference of seven percentage points.

Nearly as important as recommending action to the pastor, almost nine in ten pastoral councils said that setting the vision for the parish is a function of the council that is at least "somewhat" important to the parish. Close to two-thirds (63 percent) see this planning function as "very" important to the parish. However, only about half (51 percent) say that the council is "very" involved in setting the vision for the parish — a difference of 12 percentage points.

Two other planning functions of the pastoral council — planning for pastoral needs and developing parish policy — are seen as at least "somewhat" important by about 85 percent of responding councils and as "very" important by more than half. However, only about four in ten report that the council is "very" involved in planning for pastoral needs and in developing parish policy — a difference of 13 percentage points.

Finally, about eight in ten responding councils say that studying issues in-depth is a function of the council that is at least "somewhat" important to the parish and three in four say that the council is at least "somewhat" involved in this function. Although only 40 percent see this as a "very" important function of the council, more than a third (35 percent) say that the council is "very" involved in studying issues in-depth — a difference of only five percentage points.

The **communicating** functions of the parish pastoral council are just as important to the parish as its planning functions. These communicating functions that emerged from the survey questions include serving as a parish sounding board for parishioners, for the pastor and staff, and for parish groups. (See Table 5.4.) These functions were seen as at least "somewhat" important to the parish by 85 percent or more of responding councils and eight in ten said the council is at least "somewhat" involved in each of these. Between half and close to 60 percent said each of these functions is "very" important and between 40 and 50 percent said the pastoral council is "very" involved — a difference of only eight or nine percentage points. In other words, serving as a parish sounding board is an important function of the council and one in which most pastoral councils are at least "somewhat" involved.

We noted in Chapter Two that there are two schools of thought as to the most important purpose and function of parish pastoral councils. Some say that their primary purpose is pastoral planning, while others suggest that their primary purpose is **coordinating** the activities of parish committees. With one exception, the councils participating in this study evaluate their planning functions as more important to the parish than their coordinating functions. Developing a parish sense of community is the only coordinating function that more than half of responding councils say is "very" important to the parish. (See Table 5.5.)

Nine in ten councils agree that developing a parish sense of community is an important coordinating function. While close to six in ten (58 percent) say this is "very" important, half say the council is "very" involved in this function — a difference of eight percentage points. Other coordinating functions that three in four councils agree are at least "somewhat" important include coordinating parish activities, facilitating communication, and evaluating parish programs. About two in three agree that the pastoral council is involved in each of these.

In general, these coordinating functions of the pastoral council are apparently less valued than its planning or communicating functions, and the council is correspondingly less involved in these activities. For example, fewer than four in ten councils (38 percent) say that facilitating communication among groups is a function of the council that is "very" important to the parish and just over a quarter (26 percent) say that the council is "very" involved in this function — a difference of 12 percentage points.

Table 5.5 Parish Pastoral Council Coordinating Functions

	Percent Important		Percent Involved		
	Somewhat	Very	Somewhat	Very	Difference
Developing Parish Community	40%	58%	34%	50%	-8
Coordinating Parish Activities	34	42	36	31	-11
Facilitating Communication	38	38	42	26	-12
Evaluating Parish Programs	32	41	41	28	-13

Table 5.6 Communication of Parish Finance Council Minutes to Parishioners

	Percentage of PFCs Responding
Available on Request	40%
Parish Bulletin	16
Posted on Parish Grounds	9
Parish Web Site	3
Parish Newsletter	2
Mailed to Homes	1
Minutes not Shared	48

The Parish Finance Council and Parish Communications

As important as it is that there are frequent, in-depth, and two-way communications between the parish pastoral council and parishioners, it is perhaps even more critical that such communication exist between the parish finance council and parishioners. We have seen that Canon Law states that each parish is to have a finance council. Canon Law also requires that parishes be accountable and transparent in their financial dealings, and communicate with parishioners on financial matters:

> "Administrators are to render an account to the faithful concerning the goods offered by the faithful to the Church, according to the norms determined by particular law" (Canon 1287§2).

Supporting the Canon Law requirement is an emerging awareness of the need at all levels of the Church to tighten financial controls in the wake of a series of reported frauds carried out by both the laity and clergy, as described in Chapter Four.

From 2002 through 2005, the Washington, D.C.-based organization Foundations and Donors Interested in Catholic Activities (FADICA) partnered with Villanova University's Center for the Study of Church Management to conduct a series of national surveys of regular Mass-attending Catholics on topics related to church finances. The 2005 survey found that two-thirds of this sample agreed that the Church needs to be more accountable on its finances. Fewer than half (46 percent) agreed with the statement, "I have an adequate understanding of how my contributions to the Catholic Church are used."

We can evaluate the level of communication between parish finance councils and parishioners on three levels: the availability of parish finance council minutes, the ability of parishioners to participate in the budgetary process, and the distribution of the final budget to parishioners.

Availability of Parish Finance Council Minutes

We asked our respondents about their use of a variety of methods to communicate parish finance council activities by making the council's minutes available to parishioners. Our findings are found in Table 5.6. Parishes could report that they employ more than one method to distribute council minutes. Twelve percent of the parish finance councils in our survey made their minutes available through more than one outlet.

Nearly half of the parishes in the sample never share parish finance council minutes with parishioners. Of those that do distribute council minutes, only a handful are proactive in ensuring that every parishioner has easy access to them, either by mailing them to parishioners' homes (separately or contained in the parish newsletter) or by posting them on the parish website. One in six makes them available to those parishioners who attend Mass on a particular Sunday by including them in the parish bulletin. A large number of parishes distribute the finance council minutes in a more passive manner, posting the minutes on the parish grounds and/or providing them on request.

Parishioners' Ability to Participate in the Budgetary Process

In the era of "pray, pay, and obey" Catholics, parishioners were content to allow the parish leadership to establish the parish budget with no input from parishioners. However, that has changed in recent years. As the FADICA study cited above indicated, more parishioners are expecting to be informed and consulted on major parish decisions, including the establishment of the annual parish budget. Some, of course, believe that they should have the final say on the budget. They confuse the "priesthood of the laity" with a notion of "the pastorate of the laity." However, most parishioners recognize that Canon Law reserves the final decision on all parish matters, including the annual budget, to the pastor and are glad to let the pastor have the final say. But they expect some level of information sharing and consultation.

In fact, another survey also conducted in 2005 asked U.S. Catholics their opinion of the appropriate role for parishioners with respect to parish finances. That study found, too, that most Catholics (63 percent) think that parishioners should have some input in determining the budget, with the priest having the final say. About one in five (18 percent) are of the opinion that parishioners should have only general oversight of the finances — the priest alone should be responsible for parish finances, but he should report those finances to the parishioners. Very few, only 3 percent, think that parishioners should have no role in parish financial decisions (D'Antonio et al., 2007).

Table 5.7 displays our findings about parishioners' role in conjunction with the parish finance council in establishing the annual budget.

About three-fourths of the parish finance councils in our sample included the various ministries in the process by requesting them to submit their budgetary requests for the upcoming year. Employing this "bottom-up" approach is a sound practice, typical

Table 5.7 Communication with Parishioners in Budget Preparation

	Percentage of PFCs Responding
Ask Ministries for Budget Request	76%
Preliminary Budget Presented to PPC	49
Preliminary Budget Explained in Bulletin	14
Preliminary Budget Explained at Mass	10
Hold Open Parish Budget Hearings	9
Preliminary Budget Presented to Parish	4
Preliminary Budget Explained in Newsletter	4
Preliminary Budget Mailed to Homes	4
No Opportunity for Typical Parishioner to View Preliminary Budget	60

in nearly every organization, and it makes one wonder why one-quarter of the parishes in the sample do not practice this basic principle, and how they can ascertain each ministry's budget needs.

About half of the parish finance councils in the sample share a preliminary version of the parish budget with the parish pastoral council, before approving a final version. Again, this is a sound practice, since presumably the pastoral council (whether it is a planning council or a council of ministries) contains individuals who have an understanding of the parish and its needs and priorities. And, once again, the question is, why don't the other half of the parish finance councils in the sample arrange to receive feedback on the budget from the parish pastoral council before approving a final version?

But soliciting budget information from each ministry, and presenting a preliminary version of the budget to the parish pastoral council, will only touch a small minority of parishioners in a typical parish. Unfortunately, 60 percent of the parish finance councils in our sample do not open the budgetary process to provide all parishioners, including those who are not members of the parish pastoral council, with any information on the preliminary budget or opportunity to comment before final decisions on the budget are made.   Only 9 percent provide more than one opportunity for parishioners to receive information on the preliminary version of the parish budget.

Perhaps the best way to provide parishioners with a consultative voice is to hold open hearings as the budget is being formed. Some parishes allow parishioners to attend open meetings at which the individual ministries present their requests for next year's budget to the parish finance council. Other parishes sponsor open "town-hall-type" meetings where the preliminary budget is presented to parishioners and they are encouraged to comment on it in an open forum. In the 2005 FADICA survey mentioned above, 80 percent of regular Mass-attending Catholics agreed that parishes should sponsor open forums for parishioners where the parish's financial planning can be discussed. However, fewer than 10 percent of the parish finance councils in our sample hold open parish hearings on the budget. An even smaller number (4 percent) provided the opportunity for open meetings to discuss the preliminary version of the parish budget.

Only a small minority (4 percent) of parish finance councils take a proactive approach and mail the preliminary budget (either by itself or contained in the parish newsletter) directly to parishioners' homes. Some make certain that those who were at Mass on a particular Sunday were made aware of the preliminary budget by explaining it at some point during the Mass (10 percent) or including an explanation in the bulletin (14 percent). However, these approaches fail to reach those parishioners who were not at Mass on that particular Sunday, for whatever reason.

Communication of the Parish Budget to Parishioners

The parish finance councils in our sample on the whole did a much better job of distributing the final version of the budget to parishioners. The results are contained in Table 5.8. Respondents were allowed to indicate more than one way in which they distribute the final parish budget to parishioners.

Only about 1 percent of the finance councils in our sample failed to distribute the final budget to parishioners. Of course, this

Table 5.8 Communication of Parish Budget to Parishioners

	Percentage of PFCs Responding
Parish Bulletin	38%
Oral Reports at Mass	33
Parish Newsletter	19
Mailed to Homes	19
Posted on Parish Grounds	16
Parish Website	8
Budget Not Shared	1

is to be expected since, as noted at the beginning of this section, Canon Law requires that the faithful receive an accounting of the disposition of their contributions.

The parish finance councils in our sample employ a variety of methods to distribute their budget reports to their parishioners, with 35 percent employing more than one method. The most popular method is to provide the information in the Sunday bulletin or with an oral report at Mass. But these methods only reach those who were at Mass on that particular Sunday. Much less common were the more proactive methods of mailing the final budget to each parishioner's home (either by itself or contained in the parish newsletter) or posting it on the parish website.

Communication of Parish Debt and Investment Performance to Parishioners

In addition to the parish's operating budget, transparency and accountability call for parishioners to be regularly apprised of the parish's debt and investment situation. The findings from our survey were mixed. While almost two-thirds of the parishes report the amount of their debt to parishioners at least annually, nearly a quarter report that the parish never informs parishioners about the extent of parish debt. Information and reporting on investments were not included in the survey.

Summary

This chapter explored relationships between the two principal consultative bodies of the parish — the parish pastoral council and the parish finance council. We found that while the two bodies have different responsibilities and tend to work independently of one another, it is more common for a member of the parish finance council to sit on the parish pastoral council than it is for a member of the parish pastoral council to hold a seat on the parish finance council.

The chapter also examined communication between each of these consultative bodies and the parish. In each case, we found that communication with parishioners tends to be the exception, rather than the rule. Parish pastoral councils are more open in their communication than are parish finance councils, however. Three in four parish pastoral councils announce their meetings in the parish bulletin and close to eight in ten have at least an occasional open meeting. In contrast, fewer than one in ten parish finance councils hold open parish meetings to establish budget priorities.

The next chapter will examine more thoroughly how these two deliberative bodies function as a group. It will look at the characteristics of parish pastoral councils and parish finance councils that are associated with effective group processes.

Chapter Six

Effective Group Processes
in Advisory Councils

Parish pastoral councils and parish finance councils are intended to provide the pastor with good advice and counsel, and to advise the pastor on matters relating to the best way for the parish community to carry out its mission. This is consistent with the idea of the Church as the "people of God" and the need for all the faithful to act on their baptismal call as described in the Dogmatic Constitution on the Church (*Lumen Gentium*) and quoted in Chapter One.

In order for the parish pastoral and finance councils to permit the laity to express their opinions, they have to be functioning as effective groups. The study of group process has yielded quite a bit of research on what causes groups to function effectively. The purpose of this chapter is to review the literature on what causes groups to be effective and to consider how the pastoral councils and finance councils in this study measure up to what is known about effective groups. We will also consider what characteristics in the parish or the council structures seem to associate with more effective groups as described in the literature.

The development and maintenance of highly effective and functioning groups is very consistent with the work of parishes. More and more parishes rely on staff and parishioners working in council bodies to develop strategic plans, plan and staff programs and activities, provide training, conduct research, and facilitate intra- and inter-parish communication. The new communication technologies made available in the past two decades now enable virtual groups to work between offices and across towns. What helps to make parishes vital today is their ability to create groups that are theologically grounded and are oriented to a culture of learning, continuous improvement, and adaptation. In turn, what makes people in parishes vital (parish staff as well as parishioners) is their ability to work in small groups and produce results.

Studies of effective groups have tended to consider the nature of group structure, the relationship between group structure and group productivity, how the dynamics of the group determine its effectiveness, and the ways groups develop over time (Johnson and Johnson, 2006, p. 14). This study deals with the nature of the parish pastoral and finance councils as groups and the relationship between group structure and group productivity. The survey methodology is not appropriate for interpreting the group dynamics of the parish pastoral and finance councils or the way they develop over time. These are subjects that we recommend for further study.

The Nature of Group Structure

Two aspects of group interaction are especially important to understanding how a group is structured: differentiated roles and integrating norms. Within any parish group, the group's roles and norms structure the interaction among group members. Roles differentiate the responsibilities of group members, whereas norms integrate members' efforts into a unified whole.

Differentiated Roles in Parish Pastoral and Finance Councils

Formally, a role may be defined as a set of expectations governing the appropriate behavior of an occupant of a position toward occupants of other related positions. Often such roles are assigned in a relatively formal manner, such as appointing a chair. At other times, individuals drift into various roles on the basis of their interests and skills. Once a role is assumed, however, the member is expected (by other group members) to behave in certain ways. Members who conform to their role requirements are rewarded, and those who deviate are often punished. Roles ensure that the task behaviors of group members are interrelated appropriately so that the group's goals are achieved. The roles usually are complemcntaiy in that one cannot be performed without the other (e.g., the roles of "pastor" and "parishioner"). The expectations that define a role include rights and obligations; the obligations of one role are the rights of other roles.

Integrating Norms in Parish Pastoral and Finance Councils

Norms are rules, implicit or explicit, established by groups to regulate the behavior of all members. Norms tell group members how to behave in various situations. The norms of a group are the group's common beliefs regarding appropriate behavior, attitudes, and perceptions for its members. These prescribed modes of conduct and belief not only guide the behavior of group members but also help group interaction by specifying the kinds of responses that are expected and acceptable in particular situations. Norms thus provide a basis for predicting the behavior of other members and serve as a guide for a member's own behavior.

All groups have norms, and they may be set formally or informally. Because most groups insist on adherence to the norms as a basic requirement for membership, individuals wishing to join or remain in specific groups generally follow these "rules of the game." If they do not, they soon may find themselves on the outside of the group.

The Relationship between Group Structure and Group Productivity

Using the findings of researchers, such as Johnson and Johnson (2006) and Katzenbach and Smith (1993), four types of groups can be identified: pseudogroups, traditional work groups, effective groups, and high-performance groups. The productivity of any small group depends on how the group is structured (Katzenbach and Smith, 1993).

A **pseudogroup** is a group whose members have been assigned to work together but who have no interest in doing so.

Although members talk to one another, they actually are competing. They see one another as rivals who must be defeated, block or interfere with one another's performance, hide information, attempt to mislead and confuse, and distrust one another. As a result, the sum of the whole is less than the sum of the potential of the individual members.

A **traditional work group** is a group whose members have joined to work together and accept that they have to do so. The work is structured so that very little joint work is required. Members interact primarily to clarify how the work is to be done. They seek one another's information but have no motivation to inform the other members of the group. Members are accountable as separate individuals, not as members of a team. Some members loaf, seeking a free ride on the efforts of other more conscientious members. The conscientious members may feel exploited by the free riders of the group.

An **effective group** is more than the sum of its parts. It is a group whose members commit themselves to maximizing their own and one another's success. They believe their success depends on the efforts of all group members. An effective group has a number of defining characteristics, including:

- positive interdependence that unites members to achieve clear operational goals,
- group goals stated clearly so that all members understand the nature of the goals,
- two-way communication,
- distributed leadership,
- power based on expertise,
- a decision-making process that allows group members to challenge one another's information and reasoning,
- a decision-making process that allows group members to resolve conflicts constructively,
- members hold one another accountable, promote one another's success, appropriately engage in small-group skills, and determine how effectively they are working together.

A **high-performance group** meets all the criteria for an effective group. What differentiates a high-performance group from an effective group is the level of commitment members have to one another and to the group's success. One member of a high performing team "calls the emotion binding her teammates together a form of love" (Katzenbach and Smith, 1993, in Johnson and Johnson, 20-21). This definition of a high-performance group also seems to describe the hoped for outcome of the relationship between clergy and laity found in *Lumen Gentium.*

Are Parish Pastoral and Finance Councils Effective Groups?

To determine whether the parish pastoral and finance councils were perceived by the respondents to be effective groups, one part of the survey asked respondents to report on their experience with these councils. These items were based on research about effective group practice. They asked respondents to measure the extent to which each statement described their experience with the council, using four categories ranging from "Not at all like my council" to "Very much like my council." In order to increase the validity, multiple items using different question forms were used to measure the same subjective state (Fowler, 2002, 93). Items were scored on a scale from 1 to 4, with 1 representing the response "Not at all like my council" and 4 representing the response "Very much like my council." Table 6.1 shows the percentage of respondents who indicated that for their parish pastoral council that particular item was "very much" or "a little" like their council (column 1) and "not much" or "not at all" like the their council (column 2). Table 6.2 presents the same information for parish finance councils.

To explain how the survey findings relate to the literature on effective group process, the next section presents the group process data for parish pastoral councils, followed by the data for parish finance councils. The item numbers for parish pastoral councils refer to the survey items displayed in Table 6.1.

Table 6.1 Group Processes in Parish Pastoral Councils

Item	This Is Like My Council	
	"Very Much" or "A Little"	"Not Much" or "Not at All"
1. Goals are structured cooperatively so that all members are committed to achieving them.	91%	9%
2. Goals are perceived to be imposed from outside of the group.	27	73
3. Communication is two-way, and the open and accurate expression of ideas and feelings is emphasized.	97	3
4. Communication is one-way and only ideas are expressed; feelings are suppressed or ignored.	6	94
5. Participation and leadership are distributed among all pastoral council members.	87	13
6. Leadership is delegated by the pastor; participation is unequal with high-power members dominating.	12	88
7. Ability and influence determine influence and power; power is shared.	83	17
8. Power is concentrated in the authority of the pastor; obedience to authority is the rule.	16	84
9. Decision-making procedures are matched with the situation; different methods are used at different times; consensus is sought for important decisions; pastoral council discussions are encouraged.	96	4
10. Decisions are always made by the pastor or business manager; there is little pastoral council discussion; members' involvement is minimal.	14	86

Table 6.1 (continued)

Item	This Is Like My Council	
	"Very Much" or "A Little"	"Not Much" or "Not at All"
11. Disagreement among PPC members is suppressed and avoided; quick compromises are sought to eliminate arguing.	22	78
12. Structured controversy in which pastoral council members advocate their views and challenge each other's information and reasoning is seen as the key to high-quality, creative decision-making.	71	29
13. Conflicts are resolved by agreements that maximize outcomes and leave all members satisfied.	95	5
14. Conflicts are resolved through negotiations outside the room or avoidance; some members win and some lose; or else conflict is ignored and everyone is happy.	7	93
15. Cohesion is advanced through high levels of inclusion, affection, acceptance, support, and trust.	92	8
16. The functions of pastoral council members are stressed; individuality is deemphasized; cohesion is ignored; conformity is promoted.	13	87

Parish Pastoral Councils

Goal Setting (Items 1 and 2)

Effective groups are characterized by positive interdependence that unites members to achieve clear operational goals. Group goals must be stated clearly, so that all members understand the nature of the goals. Goals must also be operational, so that group members understand how to achieve them.

Over 90 percent of the responses from pastoral councils report that pastoral council goals are structured cooperatively so that all members are committed to achieving them. At the same time, more than a quarter of the councils perceive their goals to be imposed from outside the group. Although the survey did not ask respondents to describe the source of goals imposed from outside the group, it is reasonable to assume that among those who may be perceived as imposing those goals could be the pastor, parish organizations (in the case of a council of ministries), or perhaps the diocese.

Communication (Items 3 and 4)

Effective groups employ two-way communication. Effective communication can decrease misunderstandings and discord among group members, but it depends on minimizing competition among members.

Well over 90 percent of the parishes report that communication in pastoral councils is two-way, and that the open and accurate expression of ideas and feelings is emphasized. They do not feel that communication is one-way, with only ideas being expressed while feelings are suppressed or ignored.

Leadership (Items 5 and 6)

Equal participation and leadership ensures that all members of a group are invested in the group's work, committed to implementing the group's decisions, and satisfied with their membership. Shared leadership and participation also enables the group as a whole to use the resources of every individual and helps the group to approach the ideal described by Pope John Paul II when he wrote, "All the faithful, by virtue of their Baptism, share in a proper way in the threefold *munus* of Christ. Their real equality in dignity and in acting is such that all are called to cooperate in the building up of the Body of Christ, and thus to carry out the mission which God has entrusted to the Church in the world, each according to his or her respective state and duties" (Pope John Paul II, 2003, *Origins* 33:22).

Well over 80 percent of the pastoral councils that responded to the survey report that participation and leadership are distributed among all pastoral council members. Close to nine in ten indicate that in their council, it is *not* the case that high-power members dominate; in fact, leadership is delegated by the pastor.

Power (Items 7 and 8)

In effective groups, members' power is based on expertise, ability, and access to information, not on authority or personality characteristics. To prevent power struggles, every member of the group must have at least some power to influence some part of the group work.

Just over 80 percent of parish pastoral councils in our sample report that ability and information determine influence and power and that power is shared within the group. But this is not reported as strongly as those characteristics of effective groups previously mentioned. The most common response is that this is "a *little* like my council." Respondents are more confident in reporting that power is *not* concentrated in the authority of the pastor and that obedience to authority is *not* the rule.

Because the identity of the person responding to the survey might influence the response to this item in particular, mean scores were computed for three subgroups of respondents: (1) parish leaders (including pastors, parish life coordinators, administrators, or directors); (2) council members (including parish pastoral council chair, member, or former chair or member); and (3) parish staff (including business managers, secretaries, pastoral associates, or pastoral ministers). Although the observed mean score was smallest for respondents who were staff, there were no significant differences in the scores based on who responded to the survey.

Decision-Making (Items 9 and 10)

Effective group decision-making processes allow group members to challenge one another's information and reasoning. The method of decision-making procedures should be appropriate for the needs of the situation. The method used for making the decision needs to take into consideration the size and seriousness of the decision as well as the commitment needed to put it into practice. The most effective way of making a decision usually is by consensus (unanimous agreement). Consensus promotes distributed participation, the equalization of power, constructive controversy, cohesion, involvement, and commitment.

As noted in Chapter Three, pastoral council decisions are made through consensus in 74 percent of responding parishes, by majority vote in 23 percent of the parishes, and by formal discernment in 3 percent of the parishes.

Respondents generally characterize their pastoral councils as groups where decision-making procedures are matched with the situation; different methods are used at different times; consensus is sought for important decisions; and pastoral council discussions are encouraged. Generally, the respondents report that it is *not* the case in their council that decisions are always made by the pastor with minimal member involvement, although 10 percent of the respondents indicate that is "a little" like their council, and another 4 percent believe that it is "very much" like their council.

Conflict (Items 11 to 14)

Effective groups also use decision-making processes that allow group members to resolve conflicts constructively. When they are resolved constructively, conflicts are an important and indispensable aspect of increasing group effectiveness. Controversies over opposing ideas and conclusions are beneficial for groups, because they promote involvement in the group's work, quality and creativity in decision making, and commitment to implementing the group's decisions. Controversies also help ensure that minority and dissenting opinions receive serious discussion and consideration. Members of effective groups face their conflicts and engage in integrative problem-solving negotiations to resolve them.

The scores for dealing with conflict, though reasonably high, were among the lowest among the effective group scores in this study. Most pastoral councils report that disagreement among council members is *not* suppressed or avoided, nor are quick compromises sought to eliminate arguing. On the other hand, some parishes do not see their councils structuring controversy so that members can advocate their views. The unwillingness on the part of some pastoral council members to challenge each other's information and reasoning in order to make high-quality, creative decisions resulted in the lowest effectiveness score for parish pastoral councils on this item.

Conflicts in pastoral councils are reported to be resolved by agreements that maximize outcomes and leave members satisfied. Resolution through negotiations outside the room or avoidance where some members "win" and others "lose," or resolution through ignoring conflict is less likely to be part of the council experience.

Accountability (Items 15 and 16)

In effective groups, members hold one another accountable to do their fair share of the work, promote one another's success, appropriately engage in small-group skills, and determine how effectively they are working together.

The parish pastoral councils in our sample report that cohesion is advanced through high levels of inclusion, affection, acceptance, support, and trust. The functions of pastoral council members are *not* stressed, nor is individuality deemphasized and conformity promoted.

Parish Finance Councils

We can apply the same criteria for effective group processes to parish finance councils. Given the different type of knowledge required of members of parish finance councils, which we discussed in Chapter Two (scientific knowledge, as opposed to practical wisdom required of parish pastoral council member), we anticipate some differences in group process from that found in pastoral councils.

Table 6.2 Group Processes in Parish Finance Councils

Item	This Is Like My Council "Very Much" or "A Little"	"Not Much" or "Not at All"
1. Goals are structured cooperatively so that all members are committed to achieving them.	94%	6%
2. Goals are perceived to be imposed from outside of the group.	32	68
3. Communication is two-way, and the open and accurate expression of ideas and feelings is emphasized.	98	2
4. Communication is one-way and only ideas are expressed; feelings are suppressed or ignored.	8	92
5. Participation and leadership are distributed among all finance council members.	90	10
6. Leadership is delegated by the pastor; participation is unequal with high power members dominating.	16	84
7. Ability and influence determine influence and power; power is shared.	85	15
8. Power is concentrated in the authority of the pastor; obedience to authority is the rule.	18	82
9. Decision-making procedures are matched with the situation; different methods are used at different times; consensus is sought for important decisions; finance council discussions are encouraged.	96	4
10. Decisions are always made by the pastor or business manager; there is little finance council discussion; members' involvement is minimal.	17	83

Table 6.2 (continued)

Item	This Is Like My Council	
	"Very Much" or "A Little"	"Not Much" or "Not at All"
11. Disagreement among PFC members is suppressed and avoided; quick compromises are sought to eliminate arguing.	23	77
12. Structured controversy in which finance council members advocate their views and challenge each other's information and reasoning is seen as the key to high-quality, creative decision-making.	78	22
13. Conflicts are resolved by agreements that maximize outcomes and leave all members satisfied.	97	3
14. Conflicts are resolved through negotiations outside the room or avoidance; some members win and some lose; or else conflict is ignored and everyone is happy.	9	91
15. Cohesion is advanced through high levels of inclusion, affection, acceptance, support, and trust.	92	8
16. The functions of finance council members are stressed; individuality is deemphasized; cohesion is ignored; conformity is promoted.	15	85

The results for the individual items for each parish finance council characteristics are reported in Table 6.2.

Goal Setting (Items 1 and 2)

Finance councils report a somewhat different experience than parish pastoral councils. While goals in finance councils are reported to be structured cooperatively so that all members are committed to achieving them, about a third of parish finance councils perceive that their goals are imposed from outside the group. This is not surprising, since finance councils typically are expected to issue reports on the parish's financial situation to other groups (diocese, pastoral council, parishioners, etc.).

Communication (Items 3 and 4)

Finance councils report similar communication experiences to those reported in pastoral councils, with communication being reported as two-way and not one-way by more than 90 percent of the respondents.

Leadership (Items 5 and 6)

Ninety percent of finance council respondents indicate that participation and leadership are distributed among all council members. However, nearly one in six believe that their council is dominated by high-power members.

Power (Items 7 and 8)

Finance councils report experiences relating to power that are similar to those reported by pastoral councils. Ability and information determine influence and power, and power is shared. Power is generally *not* concentrated in the authority of the pastor.

Decision-Making (Items 9 and 10)

In more than 95 percent of the finance councils in our sample, decision-making procedures are reported to be matched to the situation, with different methods used at different times and consensus sought for important decisions by most of the parishes. In about one-sixth of the parish finance councils, decisions are typically made by the pastor or business manager with little finance council discussion or member involvement.

Conflict (Items 11 to 14)

In finance councils, the scores for dealing with conflict follow the same pattern as those reported for pastoral councils, but they are a little higher. Most parishes report that disagreement among finance council members was *not* suppressed or avoided, nor were quick compromises sought to eliminate arguing. More than one in five of the parishes in our sample did *not* see their councils structuring controversy so that members could advocate their views. More typically, about eight in ten report that they challenge each other's information and reasoning in order to make high-quality, creative decision making.

Conflicts in finance councils are reported to be resolved by agreements that maximize outcomes and leave all members satisfied. Resolution through negotiations outside of the room, avoidance where some members "win" and others "lose," or ignoring conflict are not likely to be part of the council experience.

Accountability (Items 15 and 16)

Once again like pastoral councils, finance councils report that they advance cohesion through high levels of inclusion, affection, acceptance, support. They tend not to stress the council function or de-emphasize the individuality of members.

Overall Group Effectiveness Index Score

Using the individual scores for each of the 16 survey items on group effectiveness, we develop a measure of the overall group effectiveness for parish pastoral councils and for parish finance councils. We then use those measures to evaluate the characteristics of the parish and the councils that seem to associate with more effective groups.

Eighty percent of the parishes (502) reporting on parish pastoral councils provided complete responses to the 16 survey items on group effectiveness. The scores obtained on these items are added together to obtain an overall "Group Effectiveness Index" (GEI) for each responding parish. For parish pastoral councils, the average GEI score was 53.7, with a minimum score of 21 and a maximum of 64. For parish finance councils the average GEI was 55.2, with values also ranging from 21 to 64.

As we said previously, it is reasonable to expect some differences in the GEI scores between the two types of councils, based on their different types of knowledge and their different functions. Taken together, these individual scores of group effectiveness present a very positive picture of parish pastoral and finance councils as very effective if not high-performing groups. They are generally reporting group characteristics that are associated in the literature with productive groups. However, there are two sources of potential error in this conclusion. The first potential error is caused by the parishes that chose not to respond to these items, and the second potential error is caused by the perception of the person in the parish who responded to the survey.

About 85 percent of the parishes that responded to the survey about their parish pastoral councils (624) answered the survey items dealing with group effectiveness. About 15 percent did not respond to each item. We have no way of knowing whether this group chose not to respond because they did not recognize the activity happening in their council at all or whether they chose not to respond rather than cast their council in an unfavorable light.

About 82 percent of the parishes reporting on parish finance councils (628) answered the items pertaining to group effectiveness. About 18 percent did not respond. As with the pastoral councils, we cannot know whether this group chose not to respond because they did not recognize the activity happening in their council at all or whether they chose not to respond rather than cast their council in an unfavorable light.

In the next section, we consider parish and council characteristics that were *significantly* related to the GEI. "Statistical significance" is an important concept to social scientists, who want to be as confident as possible that any observed relationship did not merely occur by chance or accident. In this chapter, we use tests of statistical significance to determine for each relationship that we are at least 95 percent confident that the relationship is not one of chance or accident.

Causality is a related issue that arises in this discussion. There is a bit of a "chicken or egg" problem here. Do the characteristics and activities under study here cause parish advisory councils to be more effective groups, or is it the case that more effective groups take on these characteristics and activities? We do not have enough information in this survey to determine the answer to that question. The best we can say is that the characteristics and activities that we examine here are associated with or related to more effective group processes. We do not know if one caused the other, but we do know that these are the kind of things that characterize parish advisory councils that display effective group processes.

First we consider factors significantly associated with the GEI of parish pastoral councils, and then we analyze the characteristics significantly associated with the GEI of parish finance councils.

Parish Pastoral Councils

While it might be reasonable to expect that parish characteristics, like the number of households, location, size of annual budget, and the length of time that the pastor has been assigned to the parish, might be related to the group effectiveness index of parish pastoral councils, these were found, in fact, to have no impact. No characteristics of the parish pastoral council membership (number of members, how selected, length of term, distribution between lay and clergy members) were significantly associated with the council's effectiveness. What characteristics were important?

Parish Characteristics

Only one parish characteristic was found to be significantly related to a parish pastoral council's group effectiveness: the leadership of

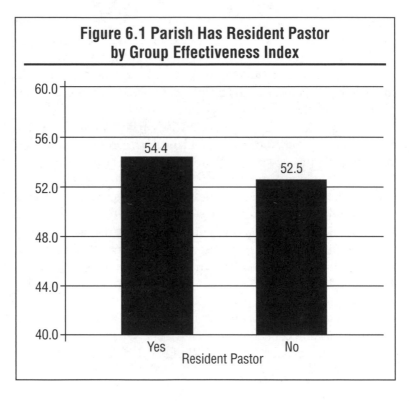

Figure 6.1 Parish Has Resident Pastor by Group Effectiveness Index

the parish. As Figure 6.1 indicates, parishes that were served by a resident priest as pastor or a parish life coordinator had a higher Group Effectiveness Index than did parishes that shared a pastor with other parishes.

Parish Pastoral Council Structure

A couple of issues concerning the way a parish pastoral council is structured emerged as significantly related to its group effectiveness.

One issue concerns the parish pastoral council's leadership. Figure 6.2 shows that parish pastoral councils that are chaired by their pastor are less effective groups than councils that are chaired by the PPC chairperson or those that are chaired by both, in collaboration.

Figure 6.2 also shows that parish pastoral councils that have formalized bylaws also function more effectively than those that do not have bylaws.

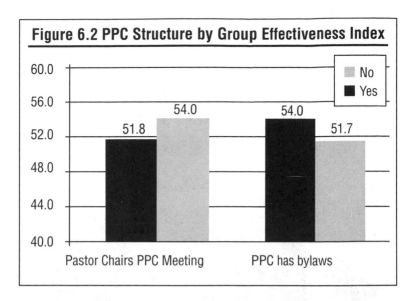

Figure 6.2 PPC Structure by Group Effectiveness Index

No / Yes

Pastor Chairs PPC Meeting: 51.8 (Yes), 54.0 (No)

PPC has bylaws: 54.0 (Yes), 51.7 (No)

Parish Pastoral Council Member Education/Formation

Are diocesan or parish education/formation programs associated with more effective group processes? For diocesan-level programs, such as providing parish pastoral council norms, orientation programs, retreats, or providing consulting to parish pastoral councils, the answer is no. On the other hand, as Figure 6.3 shows, parish-based education/formation programs are associated with more effective group processes.

Parish Pastoral Council Purpose and Functions

Recall from earlier chapters that there is some disagreement among those who study parish pastoral councils as to what their primary purpose and function should be. Some proponents (including scholar Mark F. Fischer) argue that a council's primary function is to carry out parish planning. Others view a council's role more broadly, especially those such as Rev. Thomas Sweetser, SJ, who advocates that the council should primarily oversee and coordinate parish activities.

We saw in Chapter Three that a large number of the parishes in our sample were involved in planning, but a large number were

engaged in overseeing and coordinating parish activities. Are
re differences in group effectiveness depending on whether a
ncil focuses on planning or parish activities?

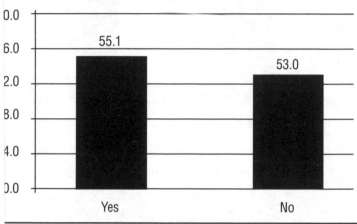

Figure 6.3 Parish-based PPC Education/Formation Program by Group Effectiveness Index

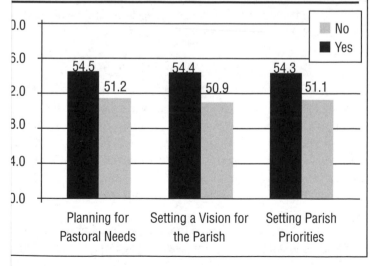

Figure 6.4 Planning, Visioning, and Setting Priorities by Group Effectiveness Index

Figure 6.4 shows that parish pastoral councils that engage in planning activities, including setting the parish's vision and priorities, are more effective groups than councils that do not engage in these activities. At the same time, Figure 6.5 reveals that parish pastoral councils that are involved in overseeing and coordinating also are more effective groups than councils that are not involved in these activities. The evidence demonstrates that both types of pastoral councils are associated with effective group processes.

Every parish pastoral council, no matter what it views as its primary function, is expected to offer advice to the pastor. As Figure 6.6 demonstrates, parish pastoral councils that recognized this role as a priority were also more effective groups.

Meeting Procedures

A number of pastoral council meeting procedures were found *not* to be significantly related to its group effectiveness. These included the frequency of pastoral council meetings, whether or not minutes were kept, and whether or not the council held open meetings. Three parish pastoral council meeting procedures, all concerned with the agenda, were associated with more effective groups (see Figure 6.7). One was including faith sharing on a council's agenda and a second was including issues on the agenda that required a recommendation or decision to be made.

Consistent with our finding earlier concerning the impact of the pastor chairing the pastoral council, pastoral councils where both the pastor (or parish life coordinator) and the pastoral council chair are jointly responsible for setting the agenda were associated with more effective groups than those where one or the other had the sole responsibility for setting the agenda. Surprisingly, regular agenda items such as council education and time set aside for evaluating the meeting were not related to the pastoral council's group effectiveness.

Decision-Making Processes

We saw earlier that there are a variety of methods that a parish pastoral council can employ to reach a decision. Some of these methods include a majority vote, reaching a consensus, or utilizing a

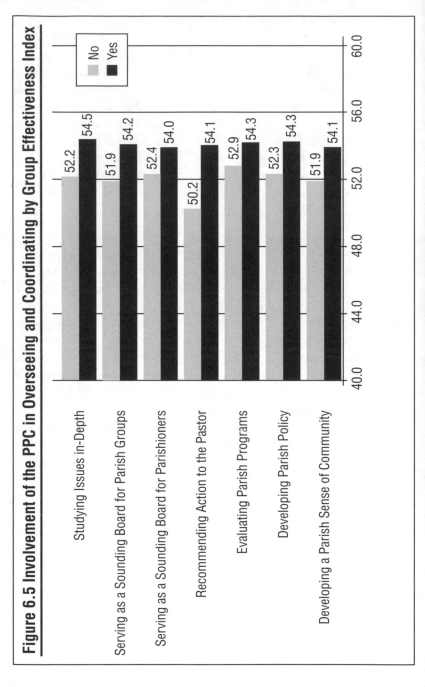

Figure 6.5 Involvement of the PPC in Overseeing and Coordinating by Group Effectiveness Index

Studying Issues in-Depth — No 52.2, Yes 54.5
Serving as a Sounding Board for Parish Groups — No 51.9, Yes 54.2
Serving as a Sounding Board for Parishioners — No 52.4, Yes 54.0
Recommending Action to the Pastor — No 50.2, Yes 54.1
Evaluating Parish Programs — No 52.9, Yes 54.3
Developing Parish Policy — No 52.3, Yes 54.3
Developing a Parish Sense of Community — No 51.9, Yes 54.1

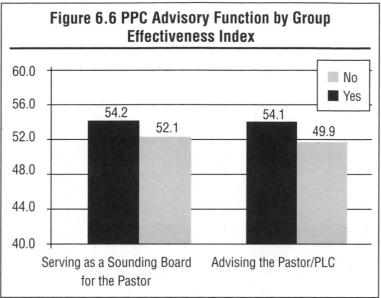

Figure 6.6 PPC Advisory Function by Group Effectiveness Index

Legend: No / Yes

Serving as a Sounding Board for the Pastor: Yes 54.2, No 52.1

Advising the Pastor/PLC: Yes 54.1, No 49.9

Figure 6.7 Meeting Procedures by Group Effectiveness Index

Legend: No / Yes

Pastor and PPC Chair Set Agenda Together: No 53.0, Yes 54.7

Issues for Recommendation/Decision on Agenda: No 51.5, Yes 53.9

Faith Sharing on PPC Agenda: No 53.2, Yes 55.0

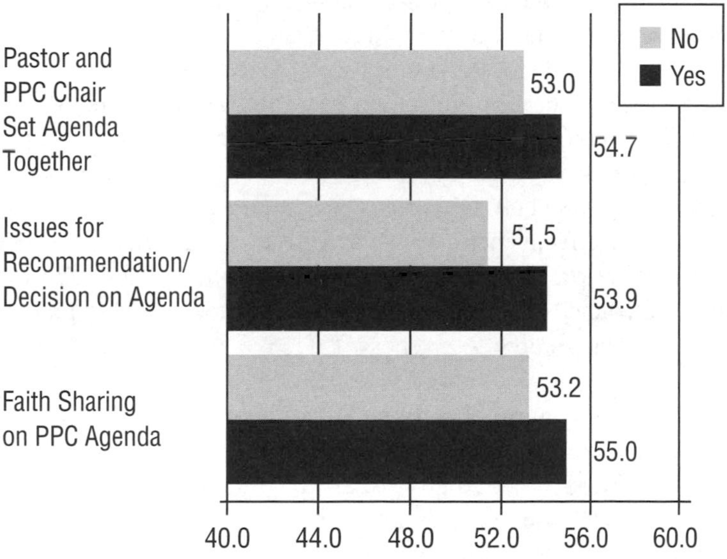

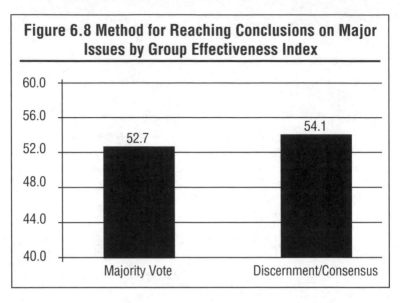

Figure 6.8 Method for Reaching Conclusions on Major Issues by Group Effectiveness Index

	Majority Vote	Discernment/Consensus
	52.7	54.1

discernment process. Not surprisingly, reaching decisions through discernment or consensus rather than by majority vote is associated with a more effective group.

In summary, parish pastoral councils that tend to be the most effective groups are those with a resident priest-pastor who defers the leadership role for the pastoral council to the council members. Parish-based education/formation programs are more likely to be associated with effective groups than are education/formation programs sponsored by the diocese or not having any education/formation program at all.

Group effectiveness is not clearly associated with either model of parish pastoral councils. Whether the council views itself as a planning council or a coordinating council made little difference as to a council's group effectiveness. Effective groups exist doing either or both of these activities.

Councils whose agenda includes faith sharing and councils who recognize that their role is to advise the pastor are associated with more effective groups, as are councils who have issues for recommendation or decision as a typical part of their agenda. Not surprisingly, councils that were more effective made decisions through discernment or consensus, rather than by majority vote.

Parish Finance Councils

As with parish pastoral councils, several factors are unrelated to group effectiveness within parish finance councils. In fact, none of the items that measure the education/formation programs provided to parish finance council members have a significant association with group effectiveness. This was true whether the education/formation was offered at the parish or diocesan level. One possible explanation for this lack of relationship could be the different type of knowledge expected of members who serve on parish finance councils. Most finance council members come to this role with the professional background needed to serve effectively.

A number of other factors, however, were found to be associated with more effective group processes. These factors are discussed here.

Parish Characteristics

As in Figure 6.9, parish finance councils in larger parishes, measured by both the number of households and the size of the parish

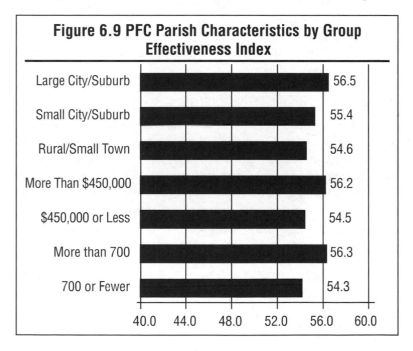

Figure 6.9 PFC Parish Characteristics by Group Effectiveness Index

Large City/Suburb	56.5
Small City/Suburb	55.4
Rural/Small Town	54.6
More Than $450,000	56.2
$450,000 or Less	54.5
More than 700	56.3
700 or Fewer	54.3

40.0   44.0   48.0   52.0   56.0   60.0

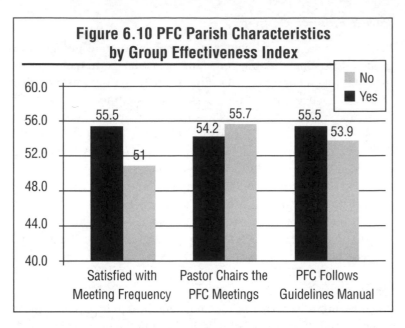

Figure 6.10 PFC Parish Characteristics by Group Effectiveness Index

budget exhibit more effective group processes. The same can be said for those councils in more urban areas. However, neither the parish's organizational structure (a member of a cluster or not) nor its pastoral staffing arrangement (resident pastor or not) is related to its finance council's group effectiveness.

Parish Finance Council Characteristics

The number of members of the parish finance council, the length of terms, and the method for selecting members are all unrelated to its group effectiveness. The frequency with which the finance council meets also is not associated with its group effectiveness, but member satisfaction with the frequency of meetings (regardless of how frequently it meets) is related to group effectiveness (Figure 6.10).

As is the case with parish pastoral councils, parish finance councils that are chaired by the pastor have **lower** group effectiveness scores.

With regards to policies and procedures, having conflict of interest guidelines had no relationship with finance council group effectiveness. Following an accounting procedures manual (whether developed by the parish, diocese, or some other agency) was also unrelated to group effectiveness. But following a policies/guidelines manual (developed by the parish, diocese, or another agency) that spelled out the responsibilities of a parish finance council was associated with effective group processes.

Parish finance councils have a number of options for communicating with the rest of the parish about their meetings by distributing their minutes. Minutes could be included in the parish bulletin, in the parish newsletter, posted on the parish website, etc. None of these communications methods was related to council group effectiveness.

Parish Finance Council Activities/Responsibilities

The two major responsibilities of parish finance councils tend to be concerned with the parish's annual budget and other financial reports that are indicative of the parish's overall financial health.

Some parish finance councils have responsibilities for other parish management activities, such as hiring/firing staff, contracting with vendors, and policing internal financial controls. Some also have financial oversight responsibility for a parochial school. For each of these, the extent of finance council responsibility is unrelated to its group effectiveness.

A parish finance council's role with respect to the budget can vary, depending on factors such as the level of involvement desired by council members and the pastor's willingness to delegate authority for the budget. The council's role can range from merely being consulted on the budget by the pastor and/or parish business manager to actually determining the budget and approving it. Parish finance councils that merely have a consultative budgetary role (Figure 6.11) have significantly *lower* group process effectiveness ratings, while those that approve the budget have significantly *higher* group effectiveness scores. In contrast, the extent to which a finance council determines the parish budget is not associated with its group effectiveness. This could signify that determining a budget can be a more contentious process than merely consulting on or even approving a parish budget, while merely being allowed to consult on the budget can be correlated with dissatisfaction with the process.

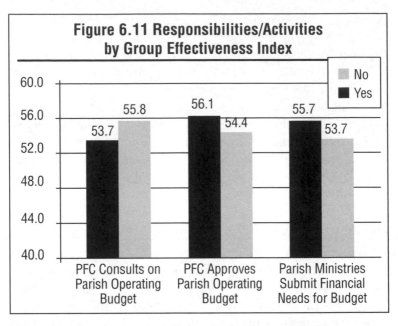

Figure 6.11 Responsibilities/Activities by Group Effectiveness Index

We asked about the effect of a number of budget preparation activities, such as holding open hearings to establish budget priorities, presenting a draft budget for parishioner feedback, and presenting a draft budget to the parish pastoral council. None of these had a significant relationship with finance council group effectiveness. The only budget preparation activity that was associated with more effective group processes was asking parish ministries to submit their budgetary needs (Figure 6.11).

With respect to other parish financial reports, we asked if the parish finance council has sufficient opportunity to review and evaluate them. Satisfaction with the finance council's ability to review and evaluate each of the following reports is associated with more effective group processes (Figure 6.12): periodic cash receipts and disbursements, year-to-date cash receipts and disbursements, amount of unpaid bills, amount of cash on hand, the balance sheet, the comparison of actual to budgeted figures, the comparison of current to prior years' figures, and the amount of debt outstanding. Or, to put it conversely, dissatisfaction with the finance council's ability to review and evaluate each of these reports corresponds to a less effective group.

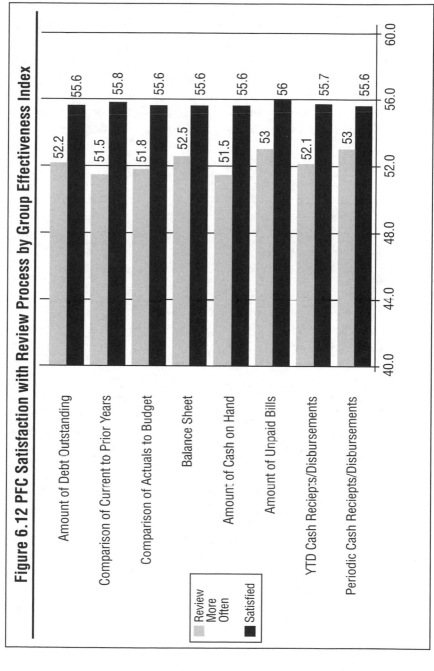

Figure 6.12 PFC Satisfaction with Review Process by Group Effectiveness Index

Legend:
- Review More Often
- Satisfied

Category	Review More Often	Satisfied
Amount of Debt Outstanding	52.2	55.6
Comparison of Current to Prior Years	51.5	55.8
Comparison of Actuals to Budget	51.8	55.6
Balance Sheet	52.5	55.6
Amount of Cash on Hand	51.5	55.6
Amount of Unpaid Bills	53	56
YTD Cash Reciepts/Disbursements	52.1	55.7
Periodic Cash Reciepts/Disbursements	53	55.6

In summary, parish finance councils in larger parishes and those located in more urban areas are associated with more effective group processes. Those that are chaired by the pastor were less effective groups. Following an accounting manual is not associated with effective group processes, but, in contrast to parish pastoral councils, following guidelines that spelled out their responsibilities *is* associated with more effective group processes. Finance councils that are required to approve the parish budget are more effective than those that actually determine the budget or are merely asked to consult on it, although receiving input from parish ministries concerning their individual budgets is associated with more effective group processes. Satisfaction with frequency of meetings and the finance council's ability to have sufficient opportunity to review key parish financial statements are all related to a more effective group process.

Other Findings

Two other survey items were included among those that were used to measure group effectiveness in both the pastoral council and the finance council surveys, although there is no research that supports any association between these items and group effectiveness. These survey items ask whether prayer is an important part of every meeting and whether the right people are on the council. The responses to these items are reported here because of their general interest.

Importance of Prayer and Having the Right People on Parish Pastoral Councils

Almost three-fourths of the parishes agree strongly that prayer is an important part of every pastoral council meeting and that guidance of the spirit is actively sought by the members. But less than half strongly agree that the "right people" are on the pastoral council. Almost 25 percent disagree with the statement that the right people are on the council.

Six in ten respondents agree that prayer is an important part of every meeting of the finance council. About the same percentage agrees that the "right people" are on the finance council.

Summary

This chapter examined parish responses to the survey items dealing with effectiveness of groups to determine if the parish pastoral and finance councils in the United States are effective groups. The roles and norms of these councils were compared with their responses to items that associate with effective groups. In the case of both the pastoral and finance councils, the responses indicate that these councils operate in a manner consistent with effective groups. The positive responses were consistent for both pastoral and finance councils. Only one area of group effectiveness was conveyed in a more marginal or provisional way. While still reported as positive, the unwillingness on the part of some pastoral council members to challenge each other's information and reasoning in order to make high-quality, creative decisions (characteristic of only 71 percent of the councils in the sample) are troubling. When the overall scores were examined to see if they differed according to who responded to the survey, no significant differences were identified.

Finally, we examined the characteristics of the councils to see if any of these are associated with higher overall group effectiveness scores. Table 6.3 shows the five most important parish pastoral council and parish finance council items associated with effective group processes, based on the Group Effectiveness Index developed in this study.

In the case of parish pastoral councils, the items related to more effective group processes are generally characteristics of the way the council carried out its business — training and forming members, including faith sharing on the agenda, and generally behaving as a planning (in contrast to a coordinating) council. The only **parish** characteristic related to more effective group process is the parish's leadership situation.

Table 6.3 Top Five Group Process Indices

	Group Process Index
Parish Pastoral Councils	
Parish-Based Education/Formation Program	55.1
Faith Sharing Typically on Agenda	55.0
Pastoral Council Studies Issues in-Depth	54.5
Council Plans for Pastoral Needs	54.5
Pastoral Council Sets Parish Vision	54.4 (tie)
Parish Served by Resident Pastor/Parish Life Coordinator	54.4 (tie)
Parish Finance Councils	
Parish Located in a Large City/Suburb	56.5
Parish Has More Than 700 Households	56.3
Parish Budget Greater than $450,000	56.2
Parish Finance Council Approves Budget	56.1
Parish Finance Council Has Sufficient Opportunity to Review Unpaid Bills	56.0

In contrast, the three most important items associated with effective group processes in parish finance councils are all concerned with parish characteristics, in particular with parish size. This could be the result of the specialized knowledge required of finance council members. Parishioners with this knowledge are more likely to be found in larger, more urban, parishes. The other two items scoring the highest Group Effectiveness Index for finance councils are concerned with council responsibilities.

It is interesting to note that none of the most important items associated with group processes for either parish pastoral or parish finance councils are concerned with the makeup of the council: how many members, how they were chosen, term lengths, etc. In general, group effectiveness is more related to council activities than to membership issues.

Chapter Seven

Recommendations

In this book we have given both parish pastoral councils and parish finance councils a thorough analysis, considering each of them from the perspective of Canon Law and the documents of Vatican II. We consulted the work of authorities on parish consultative bodies such as Mark F. Fischer and Fr. Thomas Sweetser along with experts who study issues like group processes and internal financial controls. We conducted a national survey on the practices of parish pastoral councils and parish finance councils and received over 500 completed questionnaires from each type of council.

We recognize that parish advisory councils can be complicated and controversial. Many parishioners have high expectations for the ability of these councils to enhance parish life as does the Church itself. Consultative bodies can be quite effective when employed in a manner consistent with the theology of *communio* as described in Chapter One. Their effectiveness, however, frequently depends on the ways in which the pastor chooses to use them. At the same time, every parish is different. What works in one parish may not work in another.

Nonetheless, we believe that this study has identified some common patterns that appear across various types of parishes, of all shapes and sizes, and across all areas of the country. From these common patterns, we feel comfortable in formulating some general recommendations that all parishes should seriously consider. We present recommendations for parish pastoral councils first, followed by recommendations for parish finance councils. There is no particular significance to the order in which the recommendations are presented within each type of council, however.

Recommendations for Parish Pastoral Councils

1. **Leadership Should Be Shared.** Canon 536 §1, which
   addresses parish pastoral councils, clearly states that
   the pastor is to preside over the council. However, we
   found that pastoral councils in which participation and
   leadership are shared among all members function more
   effectively as a group. These are not conflicting or mutually
   exclusive ideas. Shared leadership could include sharing
   the agenda-setting responsibility. It could even extend to
   allowing someone other than the pastor to serve as chair
   of the council while the pastor presides and listens. Even
   while sharing leadership, the pastor needs to communicate
   his vision to the council and ensure that it doesn't stray
   into areas of low priority or issues not within its span of
   responsibility.

2. **Establish Group Norms, such as Council Bylaws.** Councils
   need to establish a set of rules, either implicit or explicit,
   that regulate the behavior of all members. The norms
   reflect the council's common belief regarding appropriate
   behavior, attitudes, and perceptions for its members.
   They not only guide the behavior of council members
   but also help the council's interaction by specifying the
   kinds of responses that are expected and acceptable in
   particular situations. Norms provide a basis for predicting
   the behavior of other members and serve as a guide for a
   member's own behavior.

   All groups have norms, and they may be set formally (for
   example, 87 percent of the parish pastoral councils in our
   sample have written bylaws) or informally. Individuals
   wishing to join or remain on the council need to follow
   these "rules of the game."

3. **Provide Parish-Based Education/Formation Programs for
   Council Members.** Our survey found that in 27 percent

of the parishes in our sample, the diocese offered an orientation program for new pastoral council members and in 19 percent of the cases the diocese sponsored retreats for council members. As valuable as these programs are, we found that parish-based education and formation programs for council members are more likely to be associated with a parish pastoral council that works as an effective group. Parishes need to recognize the importance of providing their own council education and formation programs in order to help the council achieve the level of cohesion, trust, and open communication required of an effective group. Diocesan efforts might be better used to assist parishes in setting up their own council orientation programs.

4. **Include a Member of the Parish Finance Council on the Parish Pastoral Council.** As Mark F. Fischer has pointed out, the two types of councils — pastoral councils and finance councils — deal in different types of knowledge required to effectively serve in their consultative roles. For that reason, it is generally unwise to have the two councils overlap in membership, or even to make one council a committee of the other. But they do need to communicate with one another. Some items coming before the parish pastoral council will have financial implications, requiring input from the parish finance council. Likewise, the parish finance council needs to know the direction set and the priorities established for the parish by the pastoral council in advising the pastor on financial matters, such as establishing the parish budget. At a minimum, at least one member of the finance council, in addition to the pastor, should be an *ex officio* member of the pastoral council.

5. **Communicate with the Parish at Large.** Parishioners need to receive regular communications from the pastor concerning the activities of the parish pastoral council. These communications should not only take the form of the regular distribution of the council minutes, but also of

the council's vision for the parish. This communication needs to be two-way and provide the parish pastoral council members with appropriate feedback from parishioners. Parish communication is greatly assisted by the effective use of parish websites and e-mail to establish economical two-way communication.

6. **Match Decision-Making Procedures with the Situation.** We found that parish pastoral councils that rely on a discernment/consensus model of decision-making tend to be associated with more effective group processes, as opposed to those that rely primarily on majority voting. But not all issues that come before the council warrant a drawn out discernment or consensus process. In some cases, the consultative role of the council can be accomplished by a simple vote. Other issues are more complex and, in some cases, so critical to the life of the parish that the pastor is best served by having the council work at achieving a consensus on how he should proceed.

7. **Include Prayer and Faith Sharing as Part of the Agenda at Every Meeting.** As a faith-based consultative body, the importance of prayer and faith sharing to a parish pastoral council cannot be overemphasized. When included at the beginning of the meeting, these activities can set the tone for the entire meeting. It is often helpful in the middle of discussions (especially if the discussions are heated) for the council to step back and engage in prayer to help council members regain their focus as to why they are there.

This study will not resolve the question of whether the proper purpose and function of the parish pastoral council is to serve as a council of ministries or as a planning council. While the study did find that effective group process is associated with councils that set a vision for the parish and councils that plan for pastoral needs, most of the councils in this study undertake the functions of both types of councils. Perhaps it is less important whether the council views itself as primarily a planning council or a council of ministries than that the council members are in agreement that they are doing the work that the council needs to do.

Recommendations for Parish Finance Councils

1. **Leadership Should Be Shared.** Just as we recommend shared leadership for parish pastoral councils, we also recommend it for parish finance councils. Shared leadership is perhaps even more critical for finance councils, where the discussion can be expected to revolve frequently around technical financial issues, in which the pastor would likely have little background or expertise.

2. **Employ a Guidelines Manual.** Most parish finance council members would be expected to be familiar with professional financial standards such as Generally Accepted Accounting Principles (GAAP). However, parishes, as a nonprofit, are in a bit of a unique position. Furthermore, there are some accounting issues that are unique to parish life and quite different from the corporate environment. Some finance professionals may be unfamiliar with issues such as contributions to the pastor's retirement fund, the compensation of religious, or the depreciation of assets (some dioceses do not depreciate assets). There are other differences in the manner in which the Church operates in the financial arena as compared to corporate entities. Some of these issues are governed by Canon Law over civil laws and practices. Parish finance councils would be well-advised to familiarize themselves with all diocesan guidelines. Dioceses should have guidelines that are easily available to current and prospective council members.

3. **Involve Parishioners in the Budgetary Process.** Financial transparency and accountability are very important, particularly among contemporary Catholics who tend to be well-educated and financially aware. Both the study

conducted by FADICA (2005) and the book written by D'Antonio et al., (2007) confirm the importance to parishioners of not merely being informed about the budget, but having a role in its development. There are many ways to accomplish this, ranging from holding open hearings as the budget is being prepared to submitting a preliminary draft of the budget to parishioners for their feedback. But the expectation among an increasing number of parishioners is that they will have some input into the development of the parish budget. Such involvement also helps parishioners to understand and support the priority needs of the parish and is a foundation of good stewardship.

4. **Take Responsibility for Ensuring That Proper Internal Financial Controls Are in Place in the Parish.** In light of the approval of the USCCB of the report of the Ad Hoc Committee on Diocesan Audits (November 2007), it is clear that maintaining appropriate internal financial controls is a responsibility of the parish finance council. That report recommends that parish finance council members sign a statement to the effect that not only are the parish financial statements accurate to the best of their knowledge, but also that there has been no credible report of fraud or embezzlement. Basic systems, such as the segregation of duties (depositing funds, signing checks, reconciling bank statements, etc.) and the requirement for multiple signers for large expenditures need to be in place. Parish financial audits should occur on a regular basis, not only to detect fraud, but also for the protection of the parish finance council and for that of the bookkeeper as well. Some good people make innocent mistakes because they don't know or understand the correct procedure. These mistakes in the long run can be very costly. A thorough audit can be a great tool. If everything is in order, it can affirm the processes that are in place. If not, it can identify problems sooner rather than later.

5. **Review Financial Data Frequently.** Financial statements (such as the balance sheet) and other financial information (such as the comparison of actual revenues and expenditures to budgeted, the amount of cash on hand, and the amount of debt outstanding) need to be reviewed by the finance council at least quarterly. The parish finance council should be notified immediately of any dramatic changes in the parish's financial condition.

6. **Communicate with Parishioners.** In addition to involving parishioners in the budgetary process, transparency and accountability require that the pastor, after consultation with the finance council, regularly report back to the parishioners on the parish's financial condition. Quarterly reports on the basic financial data described above should be made available to parishioners. At a minimum, they should be posted on the parish website, although a more wide-ranging distribution would be preferred. A more extensive, detailed report should be mailed to every parish household at least annually. This report needs to be detailed enough to demonstrate to every parishioner the source of parish funds as well as how they are spent. Readers of this report should be able to take away from it an understanding of the parish's priorities, but it should not be so complex and detailed as to be meaningless to the average parishioner.

7. **Work with the Parish Pastoral Council to Set Long-Term Parish Financial and Physical Plant Goals.** As described in the pastoral council recommendations, it is imperative that the parish finance council and the parish pastoral council work together. This is not only important to meet current parish needs, but also in planning for future parish needs. Membership in each council requires different, but complementary, types of knowledge. This knowledge should be brought to bear in the planning process, which typically should involve financial projections.

Conclusion

In the Second Vatican Council, the Church recognized the need to engage the opinion of the laity by virtue of their baptism and in light of their competence, knowledge, and abilities. Council documents identified the organs set up by the Church as the appropriate mechanisms to do this. Canon Law establishes the requirement for parish finance councils and the desirability for parish pastoral councils. Other Church documents and statements by the Pope summarized in the first chapter further defined the important role of better structures of consultation as an intrinsic requirement of the exercise of episcopal authority within a sound ecclesiology of communion.

Most dioceses have recognized the importance of parish advisory councils, and have taken steps to encourage and support them. These steps include issuing diocesan guidelines, sponsoring education and formation activities and materials, and in some cases staffing an office specifically charged with assisting parish pastoral councils or parish finance councils. The USCCB has also been supportive, especially in the case of finance councils, through the activities of its Accounting Practices Committee. Likewise, parish advisory councils are thriving in many parishes where the laity and the clergy have recognized the mutual benefits of lay consultative groups.

Parish advisory councils are one way in which the laity can live out their baptismal commitment. The concept of parish advisory councils is still a relatively new phenomenon in the Church, and much work still needs to be done, both among the laity and the clergy, before they attain their full potential. But where they have been embraced, they have shown promise. It has been our goal throughout this study to contribute to the growth and understanding of these important parish initiatives.

References

Coriden, James. January 6, 2009. Telephone conversation with Mary Bendyna and Mary Gautier.

Coriden, James A., Thomas J. Green, and Donald E. Heintschel. 1985. *The Code of Canon Law: A Text and Commentary.* New York: Paulist Press/The Canon Law Society of America.

D'Antonio, William V., James D. Davidson, Dean R. Hoge, and Mary L. Gautier. 2007. *American Catholics Today: New Realities of Their Faith and Their Church.* Lanham, Md: Rowman and Littlefield Publishers, Inc.

Fischer, Mark F. 2003. "Pastoral Councils and Parish Management." In Charles E. Zech (ed.), *The Parish Management Handbook.* Mystic, CT: Twenty-Third Publications.

————. 2001. *Pastoral Councils in Today's Catholic Parish.* Mystic, CT: Twenty-Third Publications.

————. 1999. "What Was Vatican II's Intent Regarding Parish Councils?" *Studia Canonica* 33 (1999): 5-25. www.pastoralcouncils.com/councils-and-pastoral-planning/councils-and-planning/vatican-ii-intent/

————. 1995a. "What's Wrong with the 'Council of Ministries'?" *Today's Parish*, January:11-13, 22-23. www.pastoralcouncils.com/councils-and-pastoral-planning/purpose-of-councils/council of ministries/

————. 1995b. "Competing Visions of Pastoral Councils." In Arthur X. Deegan, II (ed.), *Developing a Vibrant Parish Pastoral Council.* New York: Paulist Press.

————. 1994a. "Should Finance Councils Answer to Parish Councils?" *Today's Parish*, March:21-23, 32. www. pastoralcouncils.com/councils-and-pastoral-planning/ purpose-of-councils/pastoral-finance/

————. 1994b. "The First Pastoral Council." *Today's Parish*, April/May: 24-25. www.pastoralcouncils.com/nature-of-consultation/historical-forerunners/jerusalem-council/

————. 1992a. "When Should a Pastor Not Consult the Council," *Today's Parish*, March:18-20. www.pastoralcouncils.com/ council-management/the-pastors-role/not-consulting/

————. 1992b. "Against Representation." *Today's Parish*, September: 23-26. www.pastoralcouncils.com/spirit-of-councils/council-membership/against-representation/

Fowler, Floyd J. 2002. *Survey Research Methods, 3rd ed., Applied Social Research Methods Series, Vol 1.* Thousand Oaks, CA: Sage Publications.

Gautier, Mary L., and Paul M. Perl. 2000. *National Parish Inventory.* Washington, DC: Center for Applied Research in the Apostolate.

Hill, W., and Gruner, L. 1973. "A Study of Group Development in Open and Closed Groups." *Small Group Behavior*, 4:355-381.

John Paul II, Pope. 1983. *Code of Canon Law.* Latin-English Edition. Translation prepared under the auspices of the Canon Law Society of America. Washington, DC: Canon Law Society of America.

John Paul II, Pope. 2003. "Response to the Assembly of the Synod of Bishops, September 30-October 27, 2001." *Origins* 33(22):353, 355-392.

Johnson, David, and Frank Johnson. 2006. *Joining Together: Group Theory and Group Skills, 9th ed.* Boston: Allyn and Bacon Publishing.

Katzenbach, J., and D. Smith. 1993. *The Wisdom of Teams.* Cambridge MA: Harvard University Press.

Lynch, John. 1982. "The Parochial Ministry in the New *Code of Canon Law.*" *The Jurist,* 42(2):383-421.

Miller, Robert. 2007. "Inter-parochial Pastoral Councils." Unpublished research report of the Emerging Models of Pastoral Leadership Project.

O'Leary, Dennis J. 1995. "Parish Pastoral Councils: Instruments of Visioning and Planning." In Arthur X. Deegan, II (ed.), *Developing a Vibrant Parish Pastoral Council.* New York: Paulist Press.

Paul VI, Pope. 1966. Apostolic Letter, *Ecclesiae Sanctae,* issued Motu Proprio implementing the following decrees of Vatican Council II: *Christus Dominus,* Decree on the Pastoral Office of Bishops in the Church; *Presbyterorum Ordinis,* Decree on the Ministry and Life of Priests; *Perfectae Caritatis,* Decree on the Adaptation and Renewal of Religious Life; *Ad Gentes Divinitus,* Decree on the Missionary Activity of the Church. www.vatican.va/ holy_father/paul_vi/motu_proprio/documents/ hf_p-vi_motu-roprio_19660806_ecclesiae-sanctae_en.html

Pohlhaus, Gaile. 2004. "Parish Pastoral Councils and the Voice of the Faithful." Presented at the June 2004 meeting of the Catholic Theological Society of America.

Provost, James H. 1999. *Theological Foundations for Diocesan Pastoral Councils: A Latin Perspective.* www.usccb.org/ laity/provost.shtml.

Rogers, Marliss. 1995. "Council Effectiveness Evaluated." In Arthur X. Deegan, II (ed.), *Developing a Vibrant Parish Pastoral Council.* New York: Paulist Press.

Sacred Congregation for Bishops. 2004 Directory for the Pastoral Ministry of Bishops. *Apostolorum Successores*. www.vatican. va/roman_curia/congregations/cbishops /documents/rc_con_ cbishops_doc_20040222_apostolorum-successores_en.html

Sacred Congregation for Bishops. 1973 Directory on the Pastoral Ministry of Bishops. Ottowa, Ontario: Canadian Catholic Conference.

Sacred Congregation for the Clergy. 2002. *Instruction: The Priest, Pastor and Leader of the Parish Community*, 26. www.vatican. va/roman_curia/congregations/cclergy/ index_en_pres_docuff. htm

Sacred Congregation for the Clergy. 1973. "Private Letter on 'Pastoral Councils'" (*Omnes Christifideles*). Reprinted in James I. O'Connor (ed.), *The Canon Law Digest, Vol. VII: Officially Published Documents Affecting the Code of Canon Law 1968-1972*. Chicago: Chicago Province of the Society of Jesus, 1975.

Shambaugh, P. 1978. "The Development of Small Groups." *Human Relations* 31:283-295.

Sweetser, Thomas, SJ, and Carol W. Holden. 1987. *Leadership in a Successful Parish*. San Francisco: Harper and Row.

Turley, Kathleen, RSM. 1995. "The Parish Pastoral Council and Prayer." In Arthur X. Deegan, II (ed.), *Developing a Vibrant Parish Pastoral Council*. New York: Paulist Press.

United States Conference of Catholic Bishops Ad Hoc Committee on Diocesan Audits. 2007. "Report to the Body of Bishops." www.usccb.org/finance/Report to Bishops Nov 07.pdf.

United States Conference of Catholic Bishops. 2004. "USCCB Committee on the Laity Report on Diocesan and Parish Pastoral Councils." www.usccb.org/laity/summary.shtml.

United States Conference of Catholic Bishops. 1995. "Diocesan Internal
Controls: A Framework." Washington DC: United States
Catholic Conference.

Vatican Council II. 1966. "Dogmatic Constitution on the Church."
Lumen Gentium, Nov. 21, 1964. In Walter M. Abbott (ed.),
*The Documents of Vatican II: Introductions and Commentaries
by Catholic Bishops and Experts. Responses by Protestant and
Orthodox Scholars.* New York: Herder and Herder.

Vatican Council II. 1966. "Decree on the Apostolate of the Laity."
Apostolicam Actuositatem, Nov. 18, 1965. In Walter M.
Abbott (ed.), *The Documents of Vatican II: Introductions and
Commentaries by Catholic Bishops and Experts. Responses
by Protestant and Orthodox Scholars.* New York: Herder and
Herder.

Vatican Council II. 1966. "Decree on the Bishops' Pastoral Office in
the Church." *Christus Dominus*, Oct. 28, 1965. In Walter M.
Abbott (ed.), *The Documents of Vatican II: Introductions and
Commentaries by Catholic Bishops and Experts. Responses
by Protestant and Orthodox Scholars.* New York: Herder and
Herder.

West, Robert, and Charles Zech. 2008. "Internal Financial Controls in
the U.S. Catholic Church." *Journal of Forensic Accounting*
9(1):129-55.

Zech, Charles E. "FADICA 2005 Catholic Donor Attitude Survey."
Unpublished research report available from Foundations and
Donors Interested in Catholic Activities, Washington, DC.

Zech, Charles E., and Robert J. Miller. 2007. "The Professional
Development Needs of Pastors and Parish Business
Managers." *Church*, 23(2):1-6.

Index

D

debt, 44, 65-66, 75, 108, 138-139, 149
decision-making, 18, 22, 25, 31, 37, 39, 43-44, 63, 96, 114, 116-117, 120, 122-124, 131, 146
Decree on the Apostolate of the Laity, 10, 12
Decree on the Pastoral Office of Bishops, 12, 14
differentiated roles, 112
diocesan internal controls, 74
diocesan pastoral council, 14
Directory for the Pastoral Ministry of Bishops, 14
discernment, 22, 31-33, 37, 39, 42, 57, 63, 120, 134, 146
Dogmatic Constitution on the Church (*Lumen Gentium*), 9, 18, 111, 115

E

education (also see formation), 25, 31, 39, 53, 58, 61, 67-68, 129, 131, 134-135, 144-145, 150
effective group, 5, 109, 111, 114-115, 120-121, 127, 129, 131, 134-138, 140-142, 145-146
embezzlement, 71-73, 75, 78, 80, 87, 148
ex officio, 29, 31, 58-59, 92, 94, 145

F

financial reports, 137-138
Fischer, Mark F., 12, 21-22, 24-25, 27-29, 31-32, 38, 41-42, 50, 129, 143, 145
formation, 12, 36, 53, 61-62, 67-68, 129-130, 134-135, 142, 144-145, 150
Foundations and Donors Interested in Catholic Activities (FADICA), 103-104, 106, 147

G

goal setting, 118, 124
group, 19-21, 26, 29, 39, 51-52, 55, 57-58, 60, 63-64, 97-98, 100-101, 109, 111-146, 150
group effectiveness, 120, 125-142
group norms, 144
group processes, 5, 39, 109, 111, 116, 121-122, 127, 129, 131, 135-138, 140-143, 146
group productivity, 112-113
group roles, 28, 112-113, 141, 145
group size, 55, 64, 69, 120
group structure, 113
guidelines manual, 80, 136-137, 147

H-J

high-performance group, 115
Holden, Carol, 25
integrating norms, 112-113
internal financial controls, 5, 19, 41, 44, 65, 69, 71-75, 80, 86, 89, 137, 143, 148
inter-parochial pastoral councils, 39
juridic person, 14

Our Sunday Visitor

Enriching Parishes...Enhancing Community

www.osvenvelopes.com

Stewardship Education:

◆ *A Steward Reflects...™* Letters
  by Sharon Hueckel

◆ *Grace in Action* Monthly
  Stewardship Resource

◆ Stewardship Pamphlets

◆ Loaves and Fishes: A Process for
  Offertory Enhancement

◆ Implementation Consulting

◆ Stewardship Conferences
  (Living Catholic Stewardship)

Offering Envelopes:

◆ Envelopes for Children and Teens

◆ English and Spanish Products

◆ Special, Seasonal and Stewardship
  Mailings for Parishes and Dioceses

◆ Catholic Stewardship Envelope Series

◆ Free Online List Manager

◆ Total Address Quality

◆ Capital Campaign Fulfillment

Our Sunday Visitor

Enriching Parishes...Enhancing Community

www.osvenvelopes.com
Toll: 800-348-2886
Fax: 800-442-0669
200 Noll Plaza
Huntington, IN 46750

Our Sunday Visitor serves millions of Catholics worldwide through its publishing, offertory and communication services. Established in 1912 by a local parish priest, Our Sunday Visitor has grown into the nation's largest supplier of offering envelopes, parish and diocesan mailings, books, periodicals, address management and stewardship services. Our Sunday Visitor is a not-for-profit organization, donating net earnings back to the Catholic community through the OSV Institute.